Virtually Disastrous

© assist Publishing 2017, Paderborn
assist Publishing is a division of assist GmbH
New edition 2017
Cover design & layout: Bookdesigns, www.bookdesigns.de
Translation support: Charlotte Weston-Horsmann
Editorial support: Tania Pellegrini

Title photo © Sergey Nivens - Fotolia.com
Publisher: assist Publishing
Printing: Tredition GmbH, Hamburg

Bibliographic information of the Geman national library (Deutsche Nationalbibliothek) : The German national library (Deutsche Nationalbibliothek) registers this publication in the German national bibliography (Deutsche Nationalbibliographie). Detailed bibliographical data may be accessed in the internet at http://dnb.d-nb.de

ISBN 978-3-9816924-3-3 (Paperback)
ISBN 978-3-9816924-4-0 (Hardcover)
ISBN 978-3-9816924-5-7 (e-Book)

Gary Thomas

Virtually Disastrous

What you really need to know about leadership over distance

My teamwork Thank You goes to:

Andrea, Kian & Zoe,
My amazing family team

and to you all at assist International HR
The best virtual team on earth

Table of Contents

"Coming together is a beginning. Keeping together is progress. Working together is success."

Henry Ford

Preface to the virtual disaster

IIIIIIIIIIIIIIIIIIIIIIIIIIIIIIIIIIIIIIIIIIIIIIIIIIIIIIIIIIIIIIIIIIII

Hand on heart: what annoys you most about your work? Until fairly recently, the answer I received when providing training or consultation in different corporations was, for the most part: "My boss, of course!" Sure, what else?

Meanwhile, the world has changed. Ever since globalisation appeared on the scene, I have been hearing responses such as: "These damn Germans!" "Those crazy Indians!" or "Not those loud-mouthed Americans again!" The litany continues with "The oversensitive British," or "Those unreliable Italians!"

The list goes on. Like I say, I hear these replies a lot, although you'll never actually find them in writing. Because what these people complain about mustn't be written down. It's a taboo subject. But how can intercultural competence be taboo?

And that's exactly the mistake. When a stiff Brit and a know-it-all German working on the same management or project team cross swords, national differences are almost certainly involved. However, if the problem persists after the second round of high-quality cross-cultural training, it might be worth considering the possibility that neither the Brit nor the German is at fault. More likely it's due to the fact that the Brit is based in one location and the German somewhere far away. So actually, it's not about nationality or interculturality, but quite simply a matter of virtuality.

Those of us who are separated by distance and connected virtually, and who, for that reason, communicate primarily via e-mail and occasionally on the telephone, are bound to run into constant friction, inefficiency and conflict, regardless of the level of intercultural competence of those involved.

We are likely to argue with our counterparts who are at a distance whether we have the same nationality or not. If you only ever communicate by email, then sooner or later there's going to be trouble! In today's globalised world it's not different nationalities that present a problem. Nationality, as problem No. 1, has long since been replaced by virtuality. Thanks to high-quality intercultural training, many well-managed and forward-thinking corporations, together with their high-ranking executives, HR departments and personnel development specialists, have got their intercultural challenges pretty much under control. This can hardly be said for the virtual challenge.

Most of those involved in virtual communication on a daily basis are rarely aware of the problem. Worse still, they tend to confuse it with interculturality. That's the real disaster. Just imagine you go to your doctor as you are coming down with pneumonia and your doctor tells you that you have a bout of summer flu. He's putting your life on the line! It's very easy to blame the symptoms of virtuality on interculturality. But it's extremely risky, as can be experienced every sunny, globalised workday. Take for example an incident in a corporation in which an Indian driver suddenly disappeared.

Not too long ago, one of the machines at an Indian plant broke down. It was such an unusual fault that consequently there were no spare parts in store. The manufacturer, who is based in Hamburg, promised immediate delivery, "immediate" meaning delivery of a 30kg part in a week's time. The CEO threatened the head of maintenance: "That is out of the question! A production standstill in India costs us two million euros per day!"

The maintenance guy panics and puts together an emergency SWAT team with his best Indian employees. They are backed up by some logistics experts from a subsidiary in Rotterdam. The team leader in Hamburg contacts customs officials throughout the country, calls up every truck driver, cargo pilot and anyone else through whose hands the parcel will eventually pass, begging them to give the shipment top priority. His counterpart in India does the same. Both parties are able to reduce delivery time to two days thanks to skilled powers of persuasion and some generous and undocumented under-the-table transactions. Teams in Hamburg, Delhi and Rotterdam neither eat nor sleep and hold their breath for two days so as not to miss the slightest movement of the parcel on the tracking monitor: now it's left Hamburg, now it's at the departure gate, now it has arrived in India, now it's at customs in Delhi. At last, the driver can pick it up! Now to get it from the airport to the plant. "Two hours max," says the Indian team leader. The members of the task force breath a collective sigh of relief and a few of them make a break for the toilets, or celebrate success with a well-earned coffee break.

Two hours later, nerves are on edge again in Germany. Three hours later India follows suit. The wires run hot between India, Hamburg and Rotterdam. Five hours later, the situation is clear: the driver has disappeared from the face of the earth! His mobile phone is dead, quite possibly due to the momentary monsoon downpour. He has no home phone since everyone in India (who can afford it) has a mobile phone. Desperation spreads: one more day will cost an additional two million euros even though the spare part is already in the country! Top management is foaming at the mouth!

It's 6:00 a.m. the next day and still no trace of the driver. Nor does he appear at 8:00 a.m. or 10:00 a.m. At lunchtime, he saunters leisurely into the cafeteria and explains: "When I left the airport yesterday, I ran straight into a monsoon storm halfway there, which caused traffic to gridlock. From experience I knew that there would be no moving forward for the next few hours, so I decided to go home first. What's the use of waiting in traffic? This morning, I had to take my daughter to her doctor's appointment and it was on the way." Two construction workers barely manage to prevent the Indian team leader, a Frenchman, from strangling the driver on the spot. The man is Indian. To this day, he cannot understand why "this strange person" got so upset. "I delivered the spare part as he ordered, didn't I? It's here now! What's the problem?"

The Frenchman is furious: "These .... Indians ...!" He vents his anger in an outpouring of choice expletives which I will refrain from repeating here. The responsible personnel development manager in Hamburg jumps to the typical erroneous conclusion: "There you have it! It's all about intercultural competence! The Frenchman should have explained the situation in a way the Indian driver would understand it! We obviously need to put our people through a few more training programmes!" What should it be? Intercultural training for €20.000? €30.000? Or why not €50.000? The task force's German team leader, whose office is a mere 50 metres away in the same building, doesn't fall for the same mistake. He has understood the real cause behind the two million euro disaster.

"Sure," he says, "our Frenchman could certainly have handled the situation more competently if he had had a better grasp of Indian culture. However, I doubt if the disaster could have been prevented in this case!" Virtuality, not interculturality, was the fire that fuelled the mishap. "In retrospect," says the team leader, "if I had been on site, I would have chosen another driver. I would have driven to the airport myself or would have realised that, by observing the driver's reaction while I was giving him instructions, he wasn't aware of the urgency of my instructions." Unfortunately, the team leader wasn't on site, nor was he in charge of a traditional team on site. He was in his office in Hamburg, communicating and leading virtually via remote control. He was leading a virtual team and using virtual communication media. Although he had already attended five cross-cultural training courses, he had never learnt how to lead a virtual team, or for that matter, how to make sure the driver in Delhi understood exactly what he was to do while giving instructions from Hamburg.

This competence gap was, in fact, the result of inadequate training and cost the company two million euros. It was a mistake that could have been avoided. In addition, management had to deal with an unhappy customer, the Frenchman with the near loss of a job, and the Indian plant with the loss of a valued worker (the Indian driver resigned shortly after the incident).

A CEO who had heard about this incredible story called me up exclaiming: "We have exactly the same problem." I assured him that I had encountered a number of companies that were faced with similar issues, but he was one of the few responsible managers who had reached the correct conclusion: "It can't go on like this!"

The problems created by virtual teams are responsible for more damage each year than Lehman Brothers, Fukushima, the eurozone crisis and Brexit all rolled into one. They cause unnecessary project delays and the failure rate to skyrocket. They hinder innovation, scare off customers, endanger careers, impair liquidity and drive team members and leaders to the verge of a nervous breakdown, normally accompanied by outbursts of, "Those damn... (Just fill in the nationality and/or company/department in question)!"

However, it's not just a problem of globalisation, cultures, nationalities or locations. It has to do with modern communication technology. Whereas once upon a time a team came together face-to-face for meetings, they can now just as easily reach consensus via telephone and video conferencing, intranet or simply by email. In other words, communication today takes place virtually. That's what IT enthusiasts would have us believe. Someone should bang their heads together, because for the most part virtual teams don't work. That's one reason why, in the past years, so many consultants, myself included, have been called upon to help develop virtual teams. "We don't get it," those in charge often tell me, "we've got our best people on this team!" This is what I have trouble understanding. After all, surely it's obvious? In virtual teams, team members:

- are dispersed worldwide in different countries and regions within a country
- speak a number of different languages and dialects
- have different cultural backgrounds
- belong to different organisations within the supply chain
- are employed by different organisations, for example in the case of a joint venture or collaborations
- have entirely different mind-sets
- have a completely different understanding of how things should work
- often have an utterly different communication styles
- have different working hours
- have to deal with different time zones
- don't see each other on a daily basis
- are not fully aware of all of these differences.

So all these major differences don't impact team leadership and performance? Of course they do. The impact on team performance is huge. Although most companies have been relying on virtual teams for years, their team leaders have never been trained in the key skills of virtual team leadership. You think that's bad? It gets worse.

Whenever I tell board members, managing directors and normal managers about the enormous challenges that virtual teams are up against, a lot of them say, "Well, I'm glad I don't have a virtual team; my four colleagues and I are in building A and the rest of the team are over in buildings D and E!" I've learned not to look too flabbergasted at such remarks. Instead I ask: "So, how do you communicate with each other when you're not attending a team meeting?" "Well, by email, of course!" Oh, and emailing is not virtual communication? So email doesn't lead to constant miscommunication across teams, creating misunderstandings and latent and/or open conflict? Even if you are just in the office next door, it takes only one email to set the entire virtual fiasco in motion.

That's why traditional on-site teams often work at cross-purposes. "We meet face to face far too rarely!" I hear from project and team leaders time and time again, even when team members are separated by a mere two floors or three buildings. This insignificant local 'separation', be it just by one floor or a scant 30 metres of corridor, manages to infect every normal team with the Triple V - the virulent, virtual virus. Although quite a few department heads and team leaders experience this on a daily basis, they have no idea what causes it. Their immediate reaction always seems to be: "Why can't they get it right?" In other words, they personalise errors made within the virtual context and blame it on individual team members: "They're just sloppy and not able to deal with conflict!" In other words, they see the fly in the soup but not the elephant right in the middle of the living room. The problem is virtual, not personal.

The teams are referred to as virtual because they are not tied down to one location. They're considered virtual because the 'location' of their collaboration is virtual. Meetings are held via Internet, video-conference or other virtual media options. Many people think this only makes a slight difference to traditional teams. Of course, traditional and virtual teams do have a lot in common. However, it's the slight difference that creates the bigger difference. Virtual teams are special simply by virtue of their virtuality, and because they are special they need a special style of leadership. The virtual team leader should upgrade his team leader licence (or have his team leader licence upgraded) a notch to include 'virtual'. That's precisely why you and I are connecting up virtually right here.

If you're a team leader, a warm welcome to you. This book was written for you. In case you think you are you 'just' a member of a team, and having read a few pages think: "You should tell my team leader this!" don't worry, I will. But until I do, please don't underestimate your own influence. As you may have already noticed, your influence as a 'mere' member of the team is considerable and clearly measurable. Bottom line: you don't have to be a team leader to steer your team toward success. Read on and you'll see how to do this.

Or if you are a manager who is above and beyond virtual teams, you have the most influence on virtual leadership, and with it, on the performance of your team. That is, if you know how to manage such teams. Read on and you'll find out.

What you will learn here will enable you to boost the effectiveness and the efficiency of your virtual teams considerably, perhaps even dramatically. Conflicts, resentment and stress will be reduced, allowing people to enjoy working together again. The feeling of permanent chaos will disappear. As a manager or team leader, you will (finally) get the respect you deserve. And quite rightly so: virtual leadership is team leadership at the extreme. Once you've acquired virtual competence and earned the virtual leadership driver's licence, you'll be able to lead anyone, regardless of the situation.

Here's where your first driving lesson begins.

Get in and fasten your seat belt.

"Myths which are believed in tend to become true."

George Orwell

1 Team Myths

ıı

The spinach myth

Virtual teams have been around for years. So have the problems that accompany them. So why are corporate leaders still calling me for advice about how to manage them? Why haven't the problems been resolved by now?

Spinach is to blame.

Even today, many mothers today still insist on feeding their children with spinach. "Here, just one more spoonful! It's healthy! It's full of iron!" Now, I'm no food analyst, but even I know that the story about spinach being rich in iron is nonsense. In 1927 a researcher put a comma in the wrong place and all of his successors copied his mistake. If I am correctly informed, spinach contains less iron than chocolate. But many people still believe the myth. That's the nature of myths. They are harder to kill than weeds in your garden. They persist despite evidence to the contrary. That's a problem. And an opportunity:

> If you find that your virtual team is not making progress, just ask yourself and your team: "Which team myth are we subscribing to?"

Here are four to choose from.

The myth of the eunuch

I know a number of people in charge within organisations, who have been complaining for years about their virtual teams' inefficiency and poor performance. Yet, they do nothing about it! Does that sound typical of management to you? No initiative and unwilling to make decisions?

Nonsense! I don't know any managers who aren't willing to look at different sides of a problem. I do know quite a few, however, who believe in myths. The sales manager of a cosmetics company speaks for many when she says: "There's no way a virtual team can perform as effectively as one whose members see each other in the hallway on a daily basis!" The virtual team is the eunuch among teams: they would very much like to perform, but they just can't. So why does the sales manager believe this?

That's simple: because that's very often the way it is. Which means that the sales manager is mistaking correlation with causality. She is privy to so many under-performing virtual teams that she automatically draws the conclusion: "All virtual teams are eunuchs; that's just the way it is!" It doesn't have to be that way. It is a myth, no more and no less. In fact, the opposite is the case:

> **Well-managed virtual teams often perform even better than conventional teams.**

When a 'normal' team calls it a day at 6:00 p.m. in Glasgow, the virtual team in Asia is just getting started due to the time difference. So, ideally, a virtual team can work around the clock because its project moves between time zones. We call this recipe for success, 'follow the sun' or 'around the clock'. A virtual project can be worked on 24 hours a day, seven days a week. Consequently, virtual teams can actually be more 'potent' than normal teams. So why do they fall short so often? Because in most cases, they are 'castrated'.

Horizontal communication is the secret of potency.

No, it's not what you're thinking! Horizontal in terms of team development simply refers to communication that doesn't take place top down or vice versa (team leaders to team members), but more importantly between team members.

A team performs when both types of communication work: on the one hand, the team leader gives clear, comprehensible, specific, goal-focused instructions from the top down, and gets useful feedback from bottom up. On the other hand, individual team members communicate with each other, for example when coordinating work packages. This ensures that team members know what the others are working on and can coordinate tasks so that work isn't duplicated, a problem which occurs often enough even in conventional teams. A lot of horizontal communication among colleagues takes place informally and automatically, on the fly, during the course of the day when they meet in the hallway, the lift, the cafeteria, in the company car park and especially around the water cooler. The crux of the matter is that if you don't run into each other on a regular basis, this automatic process is switched off. Without this, the virtual team leader has to find an alternative. If he doesn't, he'll run into the usual omnipresent virtual disaster. If he does he can make his team very successful. So do it! How? Read on and you'll find out.

The myth of mistrust

You may have noticed this yourself: in many virtual teams, there is an almost palpable atmosphere of mistrust, certainly much more intense than in conventional teams.

Quite often, once the telco or video-conference is over, the griping starts; take this example from a German-Spanish team. After the call, one German says to his teammates: "Did you hear what that Spanish guy came up with? Who does he think he is?!" By the time the next telco rolls around, resentment has built to a deafening crescendo of mutual mistrust. After three weeks at the latest, each project team member suspects that the other is up to something. That doesn't happen in conventional teams.

In a conventional team, a team member can stop by a colleague's office after the meeting and ask, "Hey, about what you said earlier: what exactly did you mean?" Ninety-nine percent of the time, outright conflict is avoided and the notion of intrigue is put to rest. Usually, it turns out the whole thing was just a misunderstanding. Informal, horizontal communication can clarify the misunderstanding instantly. Not so with virtual teams.

Nothing gets clarified. On the contrary, the Germans think of "the Spaniard" as an arrogant idiot and exchange terabytes of emails in an effort to ward off the Spaniard's devious sabotage. This, in turn, forces the Spaniard to launch into a virtual counter attack, causing the Germans to react ... and so on. Most virtual teams spend more time in a state of cyber war than getting on with work. The end result is generally mutual mistrust.

Subtle cyber-bullying is a favourite pastime in virtual teams.

The myth of mistrust states that: "Virtual teams perform poorly because mistrust kills productivity!" That's not an analysis. That's a tautology, like saying that water is wet. Of course, mistrust kills productivity! But you can't jump to the conclusion that virtual teams are productivity killers because virtuality automatically leads to mistrust! The myth claims a truism that holds only for *poorly-led teams*.

> **True: virtual teams are particularly susceptible to mistrust. As soon as trust-building measures are implemented, virtual teams are able to perform better than conventional ones.**

We will talk about building trust in teams in the following chapters.

The island myth

It gets really crazy when virtual team leaders recognise that the team is preventing its own progress due to the carefully-groomed culture of mistrust, and decide to do something about it. They request the go-ahead for trust-building measures, only to be told by the manager: "What on earth do you need that for? Forget it! Virtual teams are called virtual because there is no direct, personal contact between them due to the physical distance between them! But that's not what's important; what counts is that they get on with the task at hand and get the job done." Honestly, that's a true story. Unbelievable!

The manager's reaction reflects the island myth to a T: "Virtual team members are islands in the ocean and have no contact with the mainland. So, leave it at that!" Why do managers and employers fall for that myth?

Firstly, because trust-building measures cost money. Lots of people who can't tell the difference between an expense and an investment struggle with this. Secondly, because many bosses don't like to see their employees interacting with each other. Just consider this scene: three colleagues are drinking coffee and talking to each other. The boss stops by and says ... well, what do you think? That's right. In many corporations (thank goodness not all) all over the world and around the clock you're likely to hear: "Don't you have anything better to do? I don't pay you to stand around drinking coffee." That means that many of today's managers not only play down the positive impact of horizontal communication, trust-building and leadership in virtual teams, they actually fight against it! Unconsciously, unintentionally and without thinking of course, but nonetheless effectively.

In conventional teams this leadership flaw is not so serious. Horizontal communication takes place regardless of the boss. He can hardly monitor each and every conversation, nor can he spend all his time hanging around the water cooler. In virtual teams, unfortunately, he can. And in so doing he undermines the basic principle of teamwork: islands can't be teams, because they're isolated and not part of a network! In the next chapters we'll discuss how you can turn your isolated islands into a performing network.

Many virtual leaders start turning things around once they've seen the island myth for what it is. A department head once said, "If that's the case, why don't I invite the members of the virtual teams to our annual sales conference? As far as the costs are concerned, it doesn't really matter if we have an extra 100 people standing around drinking coffee. It will be good for the virtual teams to get to know each other on a personal level." That's exactly the point.

The one-team-fits-all myth

Problems with virtual teams are not a recent development. What do decision-makers do if these problems start to increase? That's right: they send the project managers (sometimes also team members) to team and project management training courses. On the basis of what you've learnt in this book so far about virtual teams ... does it do any good?

Yes, of course. The first two times are beneficial. And even after that, project managers can still learn something in terms of self-development. However, if your gearbox packs up on the motorway, it doesn't matter if you are able to change a tyre as quickly as the crew on Lewis Hamilton's Formula 1 team:

> **Just because a project manager knows all the ins and outs of project management, it doesn't mean he is capable of leading virtual teams!**

But it's exactly this myth that decision-makers fall for. As a result, they keep sending their team leaders to project management training. The myth says: virtual teams are like conventional teams; the only difference is that they're dispersed all over the world. That's where they're wrong!

It only makes matters worse if virtual teams are treated like conventional teams. Virtual teams are confronted with a whole set of different challenges that impact in different ways. Once you become aware of these challenges and learn to master them, you acquire a guarantee of team success. What are the challenges involved? Are there many? There are only four. In the next five chapters you will learn how to handle these Big Four Challenges.

In brief: Don't believe in myths!

- If virtual teams are falling below expectations, ask yourself: which myth have I fallen for?
- The eunuch myth says: "Virtual teams can't perform as well as conventional teams!"

- Nonsense! In principle, they can be more effective because of the 'follow the sun' advantage.
- That is, provided that you encourage horizontal communication. So do it!
- The mistrust myth: "Virtual teams perform so badly because members mistrust one another!"
- True, but that's not because of the team. It's a result of a lack of available trust-building measures. So, put some in place!
- The island myth: "The people are so far apart physically, they should just focus on getting the job done!"
- No networking? Then that's not a team. It's more like a bunch of disconnected desk drones. Get connected! Especially on the personal level.
- The all-teams-are-alike myth: "Virtual teams are like conventional teams, only further apart!"
- Okay, and an aircraft carrier is the same as a rubber dingy only with fewer paddles. Really?
- Conventional team development and project management make up the basis of virtual teams; however without virtual team competence that basis is not enough! Hunt the myths circulating in your team, among your decision makers, your clients and your management. Deflate the myths. Then and only then can you progress forward.

2. The Big Four!

|||||||||||||||||||||||||||||||||||||||||||||||||||||||||||

These are your challenges

Why do people with common sense even believe in myths (see chapter 1)? Because myths offer a sense of security.

For example, if you buy into the myth of the eunuch ('virtual teams are not capable of performing as well as conventional teams'), you don't even need to try to create a high-performance virtual team. Why should you? What's the use? Virtual teams are eunuchs after all, so why bother?

Myths offer a comfort zone. No need for challenges!

You obviously don't need that comfort. Otherwise you wouldn't be here. You are strong enough to take on the challenges of virtual leadership. Let's take a look at some of them.

Actually, there are only four, and they do stand out. If you take a look at an average virtual team, the four challenges practically jump out at you when you consider the particular features of such teams. Most often, virtual teams are separated by great distances and feel isolated. As a result, they work in solitude and are unable to develop the healthy team spirit required that could make them more productive. To make matters worse, a fourth challenge follows the first three. Very often project managers are expected to lead without authority. That's the ultimate slap in the face. Here are the four principle challenges of team leadership:

1) Create a sense of team identity!
2) Fight isolation!
3) Bridge distances!
4) Assert yourself without authority!

These are your challenges. How can you handle them? One at a time.

Create team identity!

Marie leads an international virtual team of product designers, purchasers and engineers. She has encountered problems with the team: deadlines aren't being met, redundant work packages are being delivered, and hidden animosities are hampering productivity. It takes at least three days to get responses to even the simplest requests via email, regardless of whether communicating horizontally or vertically. "It takes forever to get a response!" Marie complains. Regardless of whether she needs information from a team member, or team consensus on an important issue, she's afraid that at this rate, they won't be able to reach the first milestone. The timeline is already overextended. All this, even though the company has defined standards for performance which stipulate emails are to be answered within 24 hours. These are corporate standards. But Marie's virtual team ignores them. In time, and quite by chance, she discovers both the cause and the solution to this phenomenon.

One particularly creative designer came up with a logo for the team, which would be clearly visible on his email header for the intended 27-month duration of the project. Marie was so impressed with the idea that she began including the logo in her own emails and documents. It proved to be contagious. Within two weeks, two-thirds of the team members began using the logo. At the same time, the average time lag for emails dropped to less than two days. Coincidence? No, it's called identity. People with the same brand develop team identity. That's why teams wear jerseys and the army wears uniforms. The warriors of yore were well aware of that:

Shared symbols create a common identity.

It's a shame it wasn't Marie who came up with the idea instead of one of her team. So why are there no T-shirts in conventional teams? Well, because there is no need for them.

In conventional teams the members bump into each other on a regular basis in the hallway, in the company car park, in conference rooms and in the cafeteria. These seemingly unspectacular rituals create a sense of belonging and team identity without shared insignia. The message conveyed is: "I work here with these people. I belong to this tribe. This is my team, our project." These rituals and shared symbols are missing in virtual teams. Put simply:

No symbols – no identity – no team.

So, strictly speaking, Marie didn't actually have a team. It was more like leading a bunch of loosely designated specialists. So loose that even urgent email requests took two days to answer. "It's not my problem, it's this stupid new project." This is a typical symptom of a lack of team identity.

The logo designer had a gut feeling about this, and developed a logo that all team members could use. The more they used it, the more the team grew together, developing a sense of belonging and team identity in the process. That would actually have been the virtual team leader's job:

> **Create enough identity with the project, the goal and the team!**

Americans achieve this, for example, by distributing baseball caps, T-shirts and badges with the project name among the team members. This might sound trivial, but it does seem to work. Small gifts serve to strengthen team identity. Marie's team was able to create an initial sense of identity by using a shared logo. Committing to a common goal is another way. We'll take a look at other opportunities to develop team identity in more detail in chapter 3. At the moment, it's important that you:

- recognise the challenge of team identity.
- identify which of the symptoms of poor performance in your team are due to a lack of identity.
- commit to the ID-challenge!
- Increase awareness in your team about this challenge: "So guys, how can we create a team?"

Make sense? Ok, then let's move on to the next challenge.

Overcome isolation!

What happens when classic team meetings aren't moving forward or grind to a complete halt? People meet around the water cooler in small, informal groups and tackle issues that have come up. It's no secret that meetings are often considered "a total waste of time", harbingers of in-efficiency, and one of project management's greatest pitfalls. I've solved more problems around the water cooler than I've had hot dinners – and so, most likely, have you. Going for a cup of coffee or catching up around the water cooler ... it's all about belonging and breaking down barriers.

This is missing in virtual teams, where isolation takes the place of clo-seness. Isolated from each other around the world, team members tend to stew in their own juices. To make matters worse, project managers who lack leadership skills, whether it be with conventional or virtual teams, often feel uncomfortable with the social component involved. They don't like to see team members 'wasting' time while socialising over a cup of coffee! For some obscure reason they seem to have something against the efficiency, productivity and success that is generated upon their return from the coffee machine. If managers of this calibre try to obstruct this informal means of team development when it can be done easily, then how can they be expected to support team-building when it's really needed? Particularly in virtual teams. Instead they keep vir-tual team members in an unnecessary artificial bubble of isolation that stunts productivity and sabotages team performance, motivation and a sense of team identity. Why do some managers persist in doing that? Because they have poor social skills? Well, that may be one reason.

Just as often you hear, "There is no budget for this." Time after time, managers confide in me: "It certainly would help if we could meet on a more regular basis. But I can't get budget approval for that!" How about a team that performs poorly where members obstruct each other's ef-forts and endanger project goals? Can you get approval for that? I know, bean counters aren't willing to approve budgets for travel to face-to-face kick-off meetings because they are unable or unwilling to grasp the connection between a kick-off and the longer-term effects of long distance isolation, such as a lack of team identity and low performance. They are bean counters after all, not team leaders. They can't see what they can't see. So, enlighten them! Sell them your idea. Give them a crash course in virtual leadership.

Why not suggest a split run? Pick out two comparable projects and start one off with a kick-off and the other without. That's not exactly a scientific experiment. However, any pragmatist will be able to notice the impact that reducing isolation has on team performance. If you confront yesterday's controller with such comparisons often enough, he will change his mind eventually:

> There is no high-performance team in the whole world that has achieved top performance without personal contact (i.e. face-to-face kick-off meetings).

The Lords of the Budget will catch on to this simple yet thermo-dynamically effective basic principle even quicker if you can get support for your ideas from the top to help you break out of the isolation bubble and support your budget request. Use your powers of persuasion!

It's not that hard. Those who think pragmatically see the point: "Of course it's better if team members aren't isolated, muddling through by themselves! But given the distances, we have no other choice. We'll have to make do!" These are the kind of excuses you typically hear from managers. Not possible? Well, then we'll have to do without. The amazing thing is ... it often actually works! How come?

Because there are compensatory components that make it work. I know of a family business that, after being handed down to the next generation, continued to sell its products successfully for the next three years. They did this without a catalogue or a brochure listing their product range because the owner's daughter had studied art and wanted the catalogue to be a work of art, which never got finished. This should have been a recipe for a sales disaster. The sales team, however, were determined. They put their noses to the grindstone and they pieced together their own sales literature to compensate for the total management fiasco. That's called an operative compensatory tactic. I've rarely observed such compensatory behaviour with virtual teams because the team spirit is missing. A vicious circle if ever there was one.

Keeping team members cut off from each other results in the typical prisoner's dilemma: I'm separated from my prison mates. So instead of trying to compensate, I maximise my own individual rational benefit. As a result, it gets worse for all of us! If a manager demands, "Because of the distances involved, we'll have to make do without a face-to-face kick-off!" then he is counting on compensatory elements that don't exist in virtual teams. He oversteps the point of effectiveness of his own approach (needs must!) and is not even aware he is doing so. This is fatal, and explains the poor performance of many virtual teams.

Let's take a look at an everyday example of team communication. Kian in London sends an email to Paul in Dublin: "Where are the new drafts? You promised to deliver yesterday!" Paul reads the mail then turns to his colleague and says: "Do you know someone called Kian? Is he in this new virtual team? Take a look at what he's just written to me. Wow! Who the hell does he think he is? Just for that I'll let him wait another two days for the designs!" That's the kind of communication that takes place between people who live and work in isolation from each other.

Had Kian's and Paul's team leaders managed to overcome the isolation by inviting them, together with the rest of the team, to a face-to-face kick-off meeting, where the two could have got to know each other personally, Paul would have responded immediately: "Kian! Really sorry! I know, I promised, but all hell broke loose here yesterday. Thanks for the reminder! I'll lock my office door, switch off my e-mail and send you the drafts this evening. Sorry!" And that would have solved the problem. In the process they would also have uncovered another useless old myth.

> **The technology myth: virtual information and communication technology are effective!**

Well, they aren't. At least not where they're most needed, namely in virtual teams. The fact that Kian in London and Paul in Dublin can communicate via email doesn't mean that, thanks to the blessing of modern communication technology, isolation can be overcome. On the contrary! It becomes entrenched. Technology can't change mindsets! If it could, you could offer psychotherapy sessions from your laptop! No, exactly the opposite is true:

> **Virtual technology, great though it may be, only works once personal isolation has been overcome.**

Isolation has less to do with distance or technology and more to do with alienation and relationship building. One team leader's comment about his team was: "We haven't met each other in person – but we do have email!" Incredible though it may sound, it's something I hear from team leaders all the time. I let them muddle through for a while until they eventually call me in a state of exasperation. The issues in their teams are causing sleepless nights. Neither email nor telephone really works if there's been no previous personal contact. Of course, you'll always have the occasional genius among your team members who is able to create rapport with other team members on a personal level straight away, even with a medium as impersonal as the telephone. True, these kinds of communication wizards do exist, rare as they may be. If you happen to have one on your team, thank your lucky stars. Just don't rely on having enough of them on your team. That would be too good to be true.

Assume the norm: team members don't have a common team identity; they feel isolated from each other and develop the same range of symptoms that all homo sapiens do in isolation. They don't get on with each other. Without meaning to, they constantly tread on each other's toes when they communicate via telephone or email. Conflict is rife, whether just under the surface or outright. Team performance suffers. An avalanche of misunderstandings buries efficiency. Mistrust among team members grows. What can you do? Well, something very simple for starters:

> Recognise the isolation factor for what it is: a risk that can't be avoided by relying on communication technology. It's not about communication; it's about management.
> Tell yourself and your team: we need to manage this!

This is not some sort of New Year's resolution. It's a quantum leap in virtual team management. Up to now, most managers have tended to overlook the negative impacts of virtual isolation. Overcoming this blind spot is the first step toward eliminating virtual isolation. We'll discuss how to go about this in more detail in chapter 4.

Bridge distances!

What is the most outstanding characteristic of virtual teams? Sure, it's the distance between individual members of the team. But that's just where modern communication technology comes in! Strictly speaking, virtual teams have only come into being since technology has made them possible by dependably bridging great distances. Dependable? Don't make me laugh.

At this stage in our training courses, experienced team leaders laugh as they share their 'war stories'. One team leader, for instance, recounted: "I explained to the steering committee that we were having quite a bit of trouble communicating with Romania, whereupon a member of the board said: 'Why? Is there something wrong with the phone?'" When she told this story in the training course, the other participants burst out laughing. Only one member of the group seemed a little puzzled. This man had never led a virtual team. He didn't realise that just because Romania was a phone call away, he wouldn't be spared misunderstandings between Germany and Romania. Although the distance is bridged by technology, it isn't by communication:

> Bridging the distance within the team has little to do with technology. It's the choice of medium.

Every experienced team member realises this when finally, after several days of email ping-pong, the problem is solved quickly and easily in a five minute telephone conversation. So why not reach for the phone in the first place? Because the choice of appropriate technology is more important than mere availability.

Of course, the problem works the other way around. "The Spanish guys call me every other day and won't get off the phone!" complains the engineer based in Marseille. "Why don't they just send us an email?" Because the choice of medium had never been discussed in the team, and because the Spanish prefer personal contact.

The classic example of failure to bridge distances is video conferencing. After every video conference, senior management is convinced: "Ok, everything is clear! Let's get to work." The members of the project team who are supposed to complete their work packages based on the information exchanged in the video conference complain: "So, was that supposed to be helpful? Most of the questions are still open," and top management is still under the spell of the myth: "If it's state-of-the-art and expensive it must be good!" Or: "Because we can all see each other on screen all the relevant information gets exchanged automatically and without any real effort." That kind of thinking is naive. The team takes a different view: "Video conferencing, telco, phone call, email or files are of little use if they don't get me the information I really need!" What do you tend to believe?!

The choice of an appropriate medium is extremely important to the team's success and merits a closer look in chapters 9 to 11.

Now, let's turn to the fourth virtual challenge: power without power.

Influencing: Power without authority

Even a 'normal' project is an impertinence. Imagine you are a team leader with team members who are supposed to work for you, but they show reluctance because you are not their boss, you are a 'dotted-line manager', and you can't tell them to do anything. All you can do is try to get 'consensus'. That's what management executives and the authors of project management books often believe. In reality, however, it doesn't work that way.

Not because your team members can't reach consensus, but because for the most part, they are completely inundated with work and don't have the time for an additional project. Especially if they are assigned to three or four different projects simultaneously. Often, they are a) not really committed or b) don't accept being told what to do by someone who isn't the boss. We're all familiar with the consequences: deviations from the plan, overdue work packages. Annoyed, short-tempered team members stop meetings from progressing, if indeed they turn up at all. The team leader doesn't have the position or power to handle any of these typical project issues by giving orders or threatening disciplinary measures. He's essentially a paper tiger, a eunuch. It's precisely situations like these that led to the concept of 'Influencing' to be developed – leadership without disciplinary authority. Can it work?

It mostly works even better than leadership with power. The leader who doesn't need to rely on his position of power is the better leader in the end. Think of a stay-at-home parent who, in contrast to their husband or wife, doesn't bring home €10,000 after tax each month and yet is very much in charge. That's Influencing. Or, how about Kissinger, who negotiated a peace settlement in the Near East without a licence to tell either the Israelis or the Egyptians what to do. That's Influencing. Power is for amateurs. There is nothing wrong with power. But a true leader doesn't need that crutch to lean on. So what does he need?

He just needs the right Influencing tools. There's a treasure trove of these instruments, and you'll find out in more detail how to apply these accoutrements in chapter 6. Although you don't even need to do that. You actually already know and use some of these discreet influencing tools. For example, when you say to a teammate on the football field: "Hey, Phil, great shot!" Phil is more likely to pass you the ball next time round than if you hadn't said anything:

Appreciation is one of the most powerful Influencing tools.

The manager, Phil's team captain or the trainer have to shout instructions to Phil to pass the ball. Appreciate, and you don't need to command like that. How does that work? It's hardwired into the human brain. As the bible says: "Man (and woman) can't live on bread alone." No, we can probably survive a week without bread. But without appreciation, praise or a kind word we find it difficult to get through even a single day.

Another Influencing tool that I'm sure you're already familiar with but probably don't capitalise on in the virtual team context is sheer self-interest. Let's take a look at the following example:

Mandy: "Why haven't you devised the code for our control system yet?"

Tania: "I have got things to do you know! Your project isn't my only one! I've got four more to deal with and each one is at least as important as yours!"

"Okay, I see. What would motivate you to do our work package?"

"How about you make the specifications less ridiculously restrictive and stop treating me like a coding robot?"

"What if you were to programme the automation according to the specification but we let you be as creative as you like when it comes to the manual controls?"

"Really? That's more like it. If that's possible I'll get on it this afternoon. That's much more my cup of tea!"

Goal achieved. Thanks to conversational influencing via self-interest. The only difficult part is finding out where the team member's interests lie. That is an art form in itself. Many managers fall back on good, old-fashioned power because they haven't mastered that art. But you will. After chapter 6 at the latest.

In brief: This is your job!

- If you want the abbreviated version, you can now put the book aside since you know everything you need to know for success with virtual teams.
- You are familiar with the four big challenges of virtual leadership: identity-isolation-distance-influencing.
- Any virtual team failure can be attributed to the team leader failing to manage one or more of those four challenges.
- Few team leaders actually fail to manage those challenges. Most often they ignore them or regard them as trivial. Big mistake!
- All successful virtual teams are not successful because they have high levels of combined intelligence or market knowledge. Other teams have those qualities too. High-performing teams succeed because they establish and maintain their own identity; because they overcome virtual isolation, bridging distances; and because the virtual leader understands the art of Influencing, or leading without disciplinary authority.
- In the next four chapters you will find out exactly what you have to do to achieve this.

"Stick a suit-wearer into a pair of khakis
and he turns into an animal."

Paul T., army drill sergeant

3. The Power of Identity

|||||||||||||||||||||||||||||||||||||||||||||||||||||||||

The FBI and the invisible force

Doug, a team leader in an international organisation, leads a large team of 35 members. Because he has to give a presentation to the Board to renegotiate the team's budget, he travels to headquarters in Toulouse. Ten minutes before he's due to start, his notebook crashes. In a state of panic, he makes his way to the Board of Directors' front office. By coincidence, one of the managers appears: "Doug, c'est vous?" It's one of his team members! Within five minutes he's organised a spare laptop. Doug plugs in his USB stick and begins his presentation. In translation, the Frenchman says: "What kind of team would leave the team leader in the lurch?" Off hand, I could name at least two dozen. What kind of teams indeed? What's your guess?

Right: teams that lack the 'we' spirit. Commitment, support and standing up for one another; being there for each other and setting another member's mistakes right. Standing collectively behind one's team leader is something that only happens in teams with a strong *esprit de corps*. Most people will agree that it sounds like common sense, but it's actually quite rare. Why? Unlike a piece of office equipment, team identity is not tangible.

Identity is the single most important factor in virtual teams. It is the driving force. Unfortunately, however, it's not visible.

Former FBI agent Joe Navarro describes the impact of identity in his bestseller, *Louder than Words*. The FBI gave two agent teams the same (hypothetical) task: armed kidnappers took two innocent victims hostage – devise a plan to save the hostages! The only experimental variable was in the different clothing the teams wore. No joke!

The FBI put one group in business suits. The other team was given cargo pants and polo shirts worn by SWAT teams. Without the weapons of course. Based on the nature of the task and the background of the participants each group received, both teams should have arrived at similar solutions, options and decisions. But they didn't. Because:

In (virtual) teams the actual task is secondary. The greatest impact on team performance is identity.

What was your guess? What solutions did the teams come up with? That's right, the team in suits suggested negotiating. The cargo pants team said: "Snipers, battering ram and grenades ... storm the front door, ready to fire if necessary!" The cargo pants got the adrenalin going. While the team in business suits created the team identity: 'business people negotiate', the cargo pants team conveyed a 'here come the storm troopers' identity! Ergo:

Team identity dramatically impacts approach, performance and results. It can be influenced and formed through surprisingly simple means.

So how do you achieve that?

By distributing cargo pants?

Goals, not cargo pants

What cargo pants are for the FBI, meaningful team goals are for the virtual team leader.

So what's new about that? Every team has goals! Yes, in theory that's true. In practice it's another story. When I talk to team members about 'team goals', in most cases I hear: "I know what the particular goal of my work package is, of course, but what actually is the overriding project goal? How does this project benefit the company? How does it benefit the end user? How will things improve? You know, I'm not really sure. Maybe it's none of my business. The main thing is that the team leader knows what it's good for." Which team identity is the team member describing here? It's indifference, confusion, disorientation and apathy. No real interest, never mind identity. In conventional teams, this is not such a big issue.

In conventional teams, members are much more likely to bump into each other in the hallway, go to lunch together or group around the proverbial water cooler. These chance encounters and rituals tend to bring team members together to create the necessary, decisive sense of team identity required rather than being separated by distance and working in a vacuum (see chapter 4). All of these factors are missing in virtual teams. That's why:

Virtual teams need team goals to create team identity!

Unfortunately, many virtual leaders struggle at exactly this point because even in conventional teams the overriding team goal is not communicated clearly.

> Every team has goals. For virtual teams, however, the common goal has an almost existential significance.

A shared and clearly communicated goal is the bond that keeps a virtual team together regardless of distance. It overcomes distance and isolation. It's the common roof that all the members gather under that protects them from the rain. A common goal provides virtual team members with the basis for team identity, motivation and loyalty. Consequently, it is the best leadership tool for virtual leadership. Why's that? For one simple reason.

I'm often asked by team leaders: "How am I supposed to know if the members of my team are actually doing what is asked of them if I can't see them?" I'm sure you've already guessed the answer: it's all about a shared and meaningful goal. This is referred to as a Common Objective (CO). The more a team goal is collectively defined and formulated with a sense of purpose, the sooner you can assume (and check) whether your team is doing what is expected of them. Another frequent question is: "How do I know if my team members are doing what they should with the right level of motivation?" Same answer: a common and meaningful goal. If team members are given the opportunity to engage in animated discussion and in the end agree: "Yes, that's our common goal!" they will have generated the kind of motivation it takes to commit to this goal. Sounds obvious? In theory, yes. In practice, however, it's anything but.

When I speak of a 'Common Objective' (CO), I'm not talking about the official project goal. Every project has that, and every team member is aware of it. The parameters are often crystal clear (and, unfortunately, just as ambitious). But that's not it: if you have ten members on your team, you'll have at least eleven opinions on the project goal. For the engineer on the team the project goal is state-of-the-art development; the marketing expert envisions the "coolest campaign launch ever!" The controller has his heart set on a "project that doesn't exceed the budget." Even team amateurs know this. It's common knowledge. The professional, however, uses this knowledge as an advantage.

He asks his people directly: "In your opinion, what is the goal of this project?" Everyone gets a chance to respond by posting a message on the (virtual) pin board. He then facilitates a lively discussion in which the group identify and develop together the common denominator for the many divergent and individual goals. What they come up with is: yep, that's right. A Common Objective (CO). There's a reason why I keep repeating this. Please take this on board: not all goals are alike. Make sure your team understands the importance of the Common Objective.

A Common Objective is not a given, nor is it handed down from above. The only way to achieve a really watertight Common Objective is by asking and involving every single team member and by facilitating discussion and exchange among all the team members. This exchange in itself creates a strong team feeling, one that many 9 to 5 teams have to do without because discussion about a Common Objective is regarded as a 'dispensable luxury'. Let's take a look at that debilitating belief.

If you're having visions, go and see a doctor

The manager of a food manufacturing company in the north of England realises how important team goals are. Since the company went global there have been numerous virtual teams at work. Hence, she releases each new project with a clearly designated 'goal orientation'.

She writes, for example, the following email to the team members on her newest virtual project: "With our new nutrient mix, we aim to conquer, in particular, the rapidly growing Health & Lifestyle market segment." How do you feel about this statement?

What do you think? Is that a successful statement of objective? Does it create a sense of team identity? Well, actually it creates irritation. Below are a few comments from her irritated team members:

- "Who exactly are these Health & Lifestyle customers? I wasn't aware that we had anything like that."
- "Conquer sounds good. But what, may I ask, are we conquering? Could she be a bit more specific?"
- "Didn't she say the same sort of thing in the last project?"
- "I think she means that the new protein bar we're developing will be the new hit in fitness centres!"

I don't know how you see it, but as manager of my own company, it makes me cringe a little when my employees have to consult a management dictionary in order to get a clear understanding of what I've said. What the managing director in our example was announcing was not a team goal, but a vision. In other words, it was abstract, pie in the sky, spaced out, nebulous. In any case, it missed the point entirely and failed to create identity. How can experienced managers run into such avoidable mistakes? Because they are usually discreetly corrected afterwards. By the team members.

At least that's what happens in conventional teams. A long-standing team member explains to his colleagues after the meeting: "What the boss actually means here is: ..." This kind of corrective action doesn't happen in virtual teams. It's rare that you see email discussions to the effect of, "What the f*** does he/she want from us?" Virtual teams don't clarify; they disintegrate. That's why it is the virtual team leader's job to clarify the objective. Does that happen in your team or, for that matter, in your company?

> Give your virtual team a cloudy vision and watch team identity dissipate in the clouds.

Of course, customers often like to use vague formulations when defining project objectives. That's a given. That means that it's up to you, as the virtual team leader, to clearly formulate a common objective (CO). And that's exactly what the team leader in the example above did. Like one team member correctly guessed, the CEO actually meant: "We'll develop the best protein-power bar for fitness and physiotherapy centres!" "Ahh!" was the general reaction throughout the team. The sense of relief as things became clearer was almost palpable. Motivation increased and the coveted sense of identity grew: "We are the team with the Super-Power-Bar!" When team members translate their manager's message into clear language, then it's more than a quick fix to compensate for a lack of managerial communication skills:

> Team objectives create more purpose and motivation when the team is involved in formulating the objective.

Please take that seriously. A Common Objective that has been passed down from above is an oxymoron, a contradiction in terms! How can something be 'common' if it comes from the top down? If members aren't asked to contribute, they're more likely to feel locked out than a part of the project. Therefore:

Creating a Common Objective is the team's responsibility.
One of its first.

Where's the best place to start? You're right again.

Kick-off!

Do we really need kick-offs? If I had a pound for every time I've heard this question, I'd be sitting on a beach under a palm tree writing this with my notebook on my lap. But I'm not. What would you answer?

Based on what you've read so far and what you already know, the answer can only be 'yes'. Virtual teams, in particular, need kick-off events. A traditional team, as already repeated ad nauseum, establishes its identity through informal networking, rituals and compensatory measures. Consequently, a kick-off can be dispensed with if you really have to. A virtual team, on the other hand, can't do without.

No one wants to hear that, I know. It's no secret that managers are often tempted to avoid the bothersome kick-off altogether. This in turn drives project management trainers and experts (and enlightened teams!) up the wall. The excuses are well known: "No time!" That's humbug, of course. Every minute of a kick-off at the beginning of a project saves the company days, possibly weeks of unnecessary delays later in the project. Another favourite is: "There's no budget for that." Aha, that's interesting. So where does the money suddenly come from when glitches in the project have to be straightened out, all because team members haven't agreed on a common strategy or been able to form a team identity? Sometimes I get the impression that there's no real interest. Except for some mega-successful companies and their virtual teams. They know the answer.

Starting without a kick-off event saves time and money in the short term. In the long term, a kick-off saves incomparably more time and money.

Word has spread about this. That's why many senior managers agree to a kick-off but at the same time, keep an eye on the budget. As a result, the low-cost kick-off version takes place via telephone conference. "So, there you go. You've got your kick-off, ok?" "Actually, no, we haven't. Of course a telephone conference saves costs. That's the advantage. The disadvantage is that a phone call can't really replace a face-to-face ice-breaker meeting where people get to know each other properly. Consequently, right from the start, the opposite of team spirit happens. This does not prevent senior management from demanding "more team spirit." You could just as well stand at a potato field in March and demand that the potatoes just pop out of the ground on command. That's not likely to happen. It's not in the nature of things.

The second low-budget kick-off version is not much better. Here you have the classic power-point presentation with the project leader giving a monologue and the boss launching into a "Hey Ho Let's Go!" pep talk. Work packages are assigned and the project plan is analysed. In the evening, everyone goes bowling together for the sake of team spirit. Now there is nothing wrong with an evening at the bowling alley, but what are the chances of finding that Common Objective (CO)? Probably pretty slim. Downing a few beers together and rolling a ball along a wooden floor doesn't lead to the creation of a CO that all team members can commit to. If they did, football stadiums and bowling alleys would by now be officially accredited among the top ten personnel development measures. That's not going to happen. Why? Clearly, because you're not going to find a Common Objective in a stadium. So, where can you find one? And how?

Smart goals

When discussing your team's different goal expectations, it's important to find a common denominator. That is one point. The other is: your shared and meaningful goal should meet specific and attainable requirements. "More turnover!" one of the most well-known 'goal statements', for example, is not a goal. It's wishful thinking because it doesn't fulfil the necessary requirements. We could also call it a 'dumb goal'. But let's stick to smart goals.

The s.m.a.r.t. method of formulating goal statements has a long track record because it's easy to remember and put into practice. As you probably know, the s.m.a.r.t. method is a classic model which is taught in just about every leadership development programme. Sadly, the impact is often lost because the power of s.m.a.r.t. goals is trivialised. The s.m.a.r.t. method offers 5 simple steps on how to overcome the shortcomings of conventional goal statements. Goals that are formulated in a s.m.a.r.t. manner motivate and create identity:

S as in specific, simple, self-initiated and self-trackable
m as in measurable
a as in attractive and achievable
r as in realistic
t as in timely and totally positive

When managers or competitors formulate goal statements, you can often perceive an undertone that clearly defeats their purpose:

- Some people continually describe necessities "We should ... we ought to ..." What's the effect? It comes across as weak, creates pressure and demotivates. It offends the A-criteria (see below).
- The next person demands: "We have to cut costs!" Okay, by how much? The M-criteria is ignored. The goal can't be measured (see below).

Most everyday goal statements ignore a number of s.m.a.r.t. criteria in one swoop. It's no wonder then that so many virtual teams waft through the ether without any sense of identity.

> Consider each letter of the s.m.a.r.t. as a booster rocket for your virtual team.

Ignite each of these rockets and you'll be amazed at how your team takes off. Are you ready for lift-off?

The S-booster

It makes me smile when a manager demands of his team: "We need to increase our market presence!" That's not a goal, it's a wish. What does "increase our market presence" actually mean? In what area? New or existing customers? Which products are meant? If the boss can't find the booster button, then you do his job and hit it for him! Turn vague goal statements into S-goals.

S as in 'specific'. Many technical projects invest a lot of time in defining and documenting specifications. It makes life easier. That time should also be invested in non-technical projects. Every project needs specifically defined goals. More turnover? How much more turnover (see also M)? In what area? By what means? By when? (see also T).

S as in 'simple'. True, management is not always renowned for communicating in simple terms. They should, however, even if it takes some getting used to. The simpler the goal statement, the easier it is to remember and live by. Good goals are formulated clearly, ideally in one concise sentence. "Oh, no problem, my people know what I mean," is something I often hear. When I ask 'the people' they say: "We have no idea what he expects from us. Why does he have to explain things in such complicated terms?" Well, because that's what managers learn to do, and that's what they're paid and promoted for. Managers need to learn and practise how to express themselves in clear and simple terms if they want to communicate in a way that boosts motivation and creates identity. Unfortunately, there aren't too many natural talents out there. Even if many believe themselves to be.

S as in 'self-initiated and self-trackable'. This aspect is especially important for virtual teams. More to the point: team goals can't be dictated, not even by the team leader. Shared Common Objectives need to be defined and monitored within the team. Because virtual team members are so far apart, a lot can go wrong before the team leader is even aware of it and can intervene. That's why:

> **Virtual teams need short monitoring intervals.**

The big picture team goal should be broken down into smaller chunks so that the team is able, willing and committed to monitoring itself. Furthermore, there needs to be an awareness of what is happening in the team from one moment to the next: does what we are currently doing help us to reach our goal? The more these smart criteria are in place, the less time, money and nerves are lost due to plan deviations and delays.

The M-booster

"More turnover!" is hardly a smart goal because you can't measure it. How much is 'more'? 10, 15, 100 percent? As the saying goes:

You can't manage what you can't measure!

In spite of this, 'goals' are set every day, the achievement of which can't be clearly measured. These are the so-called qualitative goals. In conventional teams this is less of an issue because, as previously mentioned, informal processes serve as a compensatory operationalisation of vague goals. This doesn't usually happen in virtual teams. Instead, I usually observe a "Tough shit!" reaction: "What's this about now? What exactly is it they want from us? Who cares – we'll just deliver what we think they want." That's pretty ineffective, not to mention detrimental to the creation of team identity. The fact is, virtual teams need clear and measurable goals.

But what if the customer or senior management has no idea how many more thousand pounds or dollars of revenue he would like to achieve, or for that matter is realistic? It's a question I hear a lot. The answer is simple:

Goal clarification is the mother of goal formulation.

When I'm called in as an external facilitator to moderate a team kick-off, we often spend hours formulating a clear goal statement. In complex projects, deciding off-hand: "We want X percent more of Y!" just doesn't cut the mustard. It needs to be clarified with everyone in the team against the backdrop of different scenarios. That, too, is the purpose of a kick-off, so use it to your advantage. Or, clarify your goals in a different way. But for heaven's sake, clarify your goals! Otherwise you risk laying the foundation for the failure of the project before you even start.

The A-booster

Why don't people like listening to politicians? Because politicians are 'daft'? Don't be silly now. The more mature take on this phenomenon consists of two parts: politicians (and managers) often like to express themselves in a manner that is:

a)   unattractive
b)   focused on necessity

For example, a team in charge of administration in a medium-sized Austrian organisation was tasked with 'revising data storage and archiving processes throughout the company's subsidiaries'. How do you feel about this project objective? Yawn? That's about it. That goal sounds totally unattractive! Team members were bored with the project before the kick-off got underway! The decisive turn came from one of the assistants. She said: "Every wallflower can be brightened up!" The team rose to the challenge and launched into a lively discussion. Eventually they agreed on a meaningful and very attractive goal statement: "We are creating the fastest, most time-efficient and easy-to-use data storage and archiving system this company has ever seen!" And that's exactly what happened.

Make your goals attractive!

Did you notice anything here? The Common Objective does not read: "We must...!" Nor does it mention "we ought to...!" The majority of managers use modal verbs of necessity (must, have to) that have an undertone of demand or obligation, without the slightest idea what effect these terms have on people. "Must" exerts pressure: in other words, the antithesis of motivation. And where there is no motivation, there is no identification. That's why the Austrian project team took a different approach and came up with an as-if formulation: "We are...!"

Formulate your goal as if it is absolutely certain you will achieve it.

The R-booster

Usually you have a number of different team members, and they tend to be exactly that: different. And so it goes without saying that their goal expectations are just as different: the technical specialist wants the best possible technical solution; the marketing guy wants to launch a campaign the likes of which has never been seen before; the designer wants to win the red dot award. That's all good. It's ambitious. But, if you put them all together, isn't it a bit unrealistic?

As one division head in the cosmetics industry told me, "Eighty percent of our virtual projects start off with totally unrealistic goals, because the individual team members don't achieve consensus! We need team leaders who can keep their team members' feet on the ground and define achievable goals!" Indeed. That's the high art of facilitation, as anyone knows who has ever had to dissuade an overly-enthusiastic engineer from implementing his perfect solution. Actually, the recipe for this is not difficult:

> No one likes rejection. Everyone enjoys a bit of appreciation.
> So appreciate! For each suggestion that is brought up,
> sincerely appreciate the person and his/her contribution:
> "Very good. Well done!" Do this each time a new idea is
> offered. Then ask the entire team: "Ok, how are we going to
> boil all these great ideas down into one common goal that
> each one of us can identify with and say, 'I see how my
> contribution counts,' and it's realistic at the same time?"

The T-booster

In today's business world, it is easy to assume that everything is linked
to a time or a date. Well friends, that's not how it is. During the course
of a project one continually hears comments such as: "No problem, we'll
have that wrapped up by the end of the year!" Or, "We'll tackle that next
quarter!" And then it doesn't work out as planned – once again. Why?
Quite simply:

> "Soon is not a time, some is not a number!"
> Dr. Brad Blanton

If I don't know that my train leaves at exactly 4:34 p.m., then I'll still be
packing my bags at 5:00 p.m. If there's no deadline we tend to procrasti-
nate: "What's the hurry? We still have until the end of the quarter." Then
the end of the quarter rolls around and with it the dire consequences.
Procrastination is the thief of time.

The same is true for vague statements of time such as: "We've got to
change that as soon as possible!" Agreed. But when exactly is that?

Another aspect that is often forgotten is scheduling milestones. Major projects usually have milestones, but in other projects they are often sadly lacking. That is a grave mistake because it's likely to end up like the Berlin Airport project, which resulted in a huge loss of face when its inauguration had to be cancelled shortly before the scheduled project end. That's what happens when there are no milestones, or if they aren't taken seriously. On the other hand, if milestones are an integral part of the scheduling, the deadline is five times more likely to be met, mainly because deviations are recognised earlier and can be corrected.

The second part of the T-criteria states: "Please formulate your goal statements totally positively!" That, too, is often omitted. Instead one hears: "We've got to cut costs!" Okay, but by how much? "We've got to repair these faults!" "We've got to get out of the red!" Sure, but why not envisage the goal more positively: "By December 31st, we are out of the red and breaking even!" That's totally positive.

Negative goal formulations or goals that focus on deficiency are not only wishy-washy, but also have a demotivating effect (see the letters S and M above): "I don't want to be fat anymore!" Oh dear. A better, more motivating goal statement, and one that would be easier to identify with, would be: "I'll lose five kilos and look 10 years younger!"

When team members are as far removed from each other as in the case of virtual teams, they need a motivating, totally positive goal statement that builds and maintains team spirit. A not-goal sounds threatening and defeats the purpose.

Are we making too much of a deal out of all this goal business?

Build a lighthouse!

At the risk of sounding repetitive, informal contacts are essential for team spirit in every team. Unfortunately, sharing information informally is, by nature, kept to a minimum in virtual teams. Team members have too little opportunity to meet face-to-face, and even worse, rarely see the team leader. What they can see on a daily basis, however, is their project objective. So, you decide: if this is the case, what kind of goal do you want your team to embrace? Wouldn't it be one that helps create motivation and a sense of identity and loyalty? That is exactly the purpose of smart goals:

> Smart goals compensate for many of the weaknesses of virtual teams. Smart goals strengthen virtual teams.

They are like lighthouses on a stormy sea. They provide direction, guiding ships through the storm toward the Common Objective. Above all, the sailors on the ship are highly motivated. Why is that?

Even traditional teams can suffer from a lack of motivation. Team members may know what their specific work package involves, but often have only a vague idea of the overriding objective. "That's not necessary," I sometimes hear from managers. "They only need to deliver the work packages they are responsible for." The trouble is, they very often don't deliver, or deliver with sub-standard quality. Why? Because from their point of view it makes no sense. If I don't know how my contribution fits into the bigger picture, I'll probably have a difficult time staying motivated, identifying with the project goal or, for that matter, developing any sense of team spirit. Smart goals offer the virtual leader the opportunity to create highly motivated teams by developing meaningful sub-goals for the package from the primary Common Objective. Team members will go to work highly motivated day after day because they know what they are working on. The lighthouse of the Common Objective shines its light into the smallest work package and guides team members directly into their port of destination.

Fan merchandise

American teams are well known for their tendency to promote their smart goals with fan merchandise such as T-shirts, baseball caps, badges, pins, tie pins, and stickers with the team logo or slogan. Strolling across the company campus at lunchtime it's easy to recognise: "Aha, there goes a member of team X, she belongs to team Y and that group over there is half the members of team Z." This 'fan merchandise' creates a sense of identity.

True, seen from the outside, this may look a bit odd. I hear this from many European managers: "Do we really need this American-style merchandising nonsense?" Generally, that's the manager's view from the outside. Within the team, however, the members are frustrated at having to work over distances "…and then get flak from above for sporting a harmless baseball cap imprinted with the team logo!" Note:

> Team paraphernalia is like merchandise: A Man United scarf is hardly a fashion item. Team paraphernalia serves to strengthen the feeling of togetherness, regardless of what outsiders, at any level, might think.

Don't underestimate the impact fan items have on a team's sense of belonging, identity and team spirit. Why are such simple gimmicks so effective? Because humans are partly visual and partly haptic creatures. Anything that can be seen and touched takes on much more significance. That's why such items are especially effective in virtual teams. If the team members can't see each other personally every day, then at least the team's insignia can be seen or worn to convey a sense of a shared purpose that is vital for team identity. In psychological terms, such accessories are called visual and kinaesthetic anchors for team spirit.

The impact such items have is evident every Saturday in the Premier League. Just stick a mousy and painfully shy clerk into his favourite club's football shirt and he roars like a lion on the terraces! I know it might sound odd, but this goes back to an extremely powerful, 40,000-year-old primal instinct of tribal belonging. Among our Neanderthal ancestors, if you didn't belong to a group, you were likely to be devoured by a sabre-tooth tiger within days if a rival clan didn't butcher you first. That's why a sense of belonging is such a strong instinct. A smart virtual team leader will know how to use this powerful instinct to the team's advantage.

You can enhance the sense of team identity even further by coming up with a catchy symbol and a team name. Naturally, you do this together with team members. If your team is too big for that and you find it difficult to choose a catchy team name together with 87 team members, one frequently used approach is to create a core team consisting of five to nine members.

Do you know what the turbo charger for team identity is? Photos! A large HR development organisation came across that by chance a few years ago. Two of the five virtual projects launched by an international fashion company actually had a kick-off meeting approved. The teams met for two days in Milan at the company's headquarters. The goals were clarified, planning was roughly outlined, and the milestones set. Because of the generally positive mood, all the team members came together for a photo in front of the impressive facade of the headquarters building. Every member had the photo sent to them.

All team members printed it out and hung it up in their offices. Some even had posters made. Almost all of them uploaded it on their mobile phones, and others used it as a screensaver on their personal computers and/or tablets. The project leader forwarded the picture to the team's external HR developer. When he asked what it was supposed to mean, the project leader said: "That's our little family and you're part of it!" Family? That's been the strongest team identity for homo sapiens for the past 40,000 years. My advice: just do it! If you can't get approval for a kick-off, never mind. You can achieve similar results with photo collages, where every team member sends in a photo of themselves. All the photos are then arranged together in a collage. Often one team member is skilled at image editing and can create a realistic-looking background such as some historic setting, Mount Rushmore or the Eiffel Tower. If you think this all sounds far too fluffy and sentimental you've probably never asked yourself why troops go into battle with banners waving overhead:

Insignias create identity!

So create your own symbols for team identity.

Be a great motivator!

Under what circumstances do we achieve greatness? When and why do we deliver top performance? Because we're offered bonuses or incentives? Only die-hard materialists believe that nowadays. Alexander the Great didn't conquer half the world to be rewarded with a company car. Even Warren Buffett isn't in it for the money. What has always inspired man to achieve greatness is, and always will be, outstanding ideas, common objectives and a strong sense of community.

In a co-located team, team spirit evolves informally or around the proverbial water cooler. Virtual teams, on the other hand, are faced with their very own challenge of having to create smart goals, a sense of identity and community. So take on the challenge. By now you're familiar with the necessary tools. Just put them to work! Don't worry if it doesn't work immediately. As I hear frequently from virtual team leaders who give it a try, it's well worth the effort.

For example, the division head of a chemical firm once told me: "Although the team split up eight years ago, the 17 members of the Albatross team chat almost daily and share ideas via Intranet. The project back then lasted only a year, but the 'team feeling' and the general mood was so upbeat it was addictive. That's not something you experience every day in a typical department, so you find yourself determined to hold on to it." Incidentally, the team delivered one of the most successful projects in the company's history. Not because the team was made up of the best experts, but because of the upbeat team spirit. Each team member pulled his/her weight and worked hard to deliver their best: they were committed to a common goal and created a team identity.

Team identity is not a gift. It takes hard work.

So work on it.

Advanced-level identity forming

It's not as if each team member joins the team in a state of *tabula rasa*. Naturally, we all bring our individual identities into any team we join. We also bring in elements of the group identities we experienced in former teams or from the departments that we represent in the project team. A smart virtual leader understands this and is able to merge these individual identities and other group identities with a powerful Common Objective, with which all members can identify.

Recognise existing characteristics of identity and build them into a powerful new team identity.

This is extremely important, because the existing identities continue to exist in the new team and tend to take on a life of their own. I'm sure you're familiar with the constellation of engineers vs. sales staff; sales office vs. field staff; Marketing vs. Production; Sales vs. Finance. What can you do? You can hardly forbid both latent and open conflict by official decree. As I'm sure you know, that is unlikely to work. It's something only a rookie would resort to. A professional will work with the different identities, not against them.

Integrate individual and group identities into a new whole that is more than the sum of its parts.

That requires insight, experience and clear communication. Actually, it's not that difficult. For instance, in the case of a project team leader who interrupted a routine squabble between the engineer and marketing guys in the group: "We aren't just a team of engineers or marketing experts! We're the greatest marketing and the best technical team!" Granted, that sounds a bit presumptuous. However, the response from one of the engineers was: "Exactly!" The marketing guy joined in: "I have an idea! I'll put that on a badge!" From then on, every member identified with the greatest marketing and the best technical team. The team leader had, quite simply, managed to integrate two opposing identity characteristics into an overarching whole. That's the secret behind identity-building (and world peace, should it ever happen):

Integration, not isolation!

That's the ideal situation. What does real life look like? Usually one side wins, in this case either the engineers or the marketing guys. The 'losers' are isolated and marginalised: "Hey, you engineering/marketing guys don't know what you're talking about!" That might work but it kills an awful lot of commitment, productivity and the sense of community, which usually happens when people are isolated. Isolation is a tool that beginners resort to. Professionals don't isolate, they integrate. Because they know that strong team bonding is their most powerful ally: the most important driver of performance and the decisive productivity factor on the way to delivering a successful project.

In brief: Creating identity!

- Virtual teams are much more in need of creating a strong team identity than conventional teams.
- Build and integrate team spirit!
- This is best accomplished by goal definition and goal formulation.
- Use the s.m.a.r.t. method (or any other goal matrix that covers the necessary criteria); agree on and formulate smart goals.
- S as in specific, simple and self-trackable.
- M as in measurable.
- A as in attractive.
- And in 'as if now': formulated in a way that ensures that the goal is reachable.

- R as in realistic.
- T as in timely and formulated in a totally positive way.

- Foster identity-building with fan merchandise, provided you've got the budget and it aligns with the company culture (a photo is always possible!)
- Integrate your team members' existing identity characteristics into a new team identity.

"Any person condemned to solitary confinement will
end up with hallucinations."

Christiena K., project leader

4. Avoid the isolation trap!

The prisoner's dilemma

This one's a classic, although few have heard of it: two people are arrested and accused of robbing a bank. The evidence is tenuous; only a confession can prove them guilty. So the police officer has them sit in separate interview rooms and offers each one a deal: "Blow the whistle on your friend and I'll let you go!" Of course, each prisoner immediately thinks: "If the other guy talks first, I'll go to jail! Ok, so I have to be first!" That's the solution!

Is it? Probably not. The best solution for both is: keep your mouth shut, in which case, both will be released. That's exactly what they'd do if they could put their heads together. That's why they've been put in isolation. Isolation makes people do dumb things. Police officers are aware of that, unlike a good many project leaders and their bosses, I dare say.

Isolation is the mother of all stupidity.

The prisoner's dilemma can be found in every good business school textbook. It serves to familiarise first-year students with the disastrous effect isolation has on team performance. Not only does performance suffer in this classic dilemma, but it actually blows the entire team apart (one member goes to prison). The best thing about the prisoner's dilemma is that all managers understand it when it's presented in leadership training. Straight after the training, however, they return to their offices and continue to lead their teams in isolation: a perfect example of the knowing-doing-gap, a term coined and researched by the two Harvard professors, Pfeffer and Sutton:

> The more 'trivial' an insight seems, the less likely it will be applied.

That is something that Bill came up against.

Bill's case

The members of Bill's virtual team live in different cities throughout the country. Andrea, for instance, lives in Birmingham and Stewart lives in London. One day, Stewart receives a phone call from Andrea: "Do you think you could deliver your work package a week earlier than planned? That way we could get straight into the testing lab and wouldn't have to wait the extra three weeks for another slot to open! The additional waiting time might endanger our reaching the milestone." Stewart is furious.

"Who does that stupid cow think she is? As if we had nothing to do down here! I can hardly keep up with the schedule as it is, never mind a week earlier! All because they've obviously screwed up the lab scheduling!"

Stewart refuses point blank. After all, it's not his fault that the milestone is in danger of not being met. That's when fate steps in.

By coincidence, a salesman from Birmingham who is attending a training session in London is sitting at the same table as Stewart in the cafeteria. He is about to settle down to his meal when he overhears the salesman's story: "We're all lucky to be alive. A month ago we were nearly blown out of our building because of some hair-brained lab assistant. Now the lab team is lagging behind and the scheduling is all over the place. But hey, with some flexibility and a bit of good will we can catch up." Stewart suddenly realised that it was exactly this flexibility and good will that he had refused his colleague Andrea. Because he had no idea what was going on. Because he was isolated. Because he hadn't been able to talk with his 'co-prisoners' and consequently had no idea what they were going through. The upshot, however, was that Bill, the project leader, never found out how near they had come to missing the next milestone. The situation was saved by a coincidence known as horizontal communication.

What is horizontal communication? No, don't get your hopes up. It's not what you're thinking. It doesn't happen where you think it does. Horizontal communication happens when people on the same hierarchical level communicate by whichever means are available. This usually occurs informally in the form of small talk, discussions over lunch or bumping into each other in the hallway, in the lift or around the water cooler. In fact, the term 'water cooler moments' has become a buzz word. Why? What's so great about horizontal communication?

Horizontal communication vs. isolation

By definition, virtual teams are separated by physical distance. They work in isolation from one another. As we know, isolation is a performance killer – unless horizontal communication manages to bridge the distance and release team members from solitary confinement.

In conventional teams, horizontal communication usually occurs informally. It's taken for granted. After all, team members run into each other often enough. Virtual teams don't have that advantage. That in itself is not the problem. Such challenges can be overcome. That is, if one is aware that there is a challenge. That's where the trouble starts.

This particular form of disadvantage is not only not perceived, but I have the impression many managers really don't want to see it. I had the following conversation with a member of Bill's leadership committee:

He: "I heard that reaching the milestone was in danger for a while. What happened?"
Me: "Two members didn't share some important information!"
"But they're constantly on the phone or exchanging emails!"
"True, but they stick to task-related issues."
"Well, isn't that what they're supposed to be doing on the project?"
"You're absolutely right – but that alone is not enough. If it was just about the current task at hand, the milestone would never have been at risk. It's also about the more general context information people find out in casual conversation."
"I don't want my people wasting time chatting over coffee. They're supposed to be working!"
"It's precisely what you call 'wasting time chatting over coffee' that boosts performance in virtual teams. It's called horizontal communication."
"Are you trying to convince me that standing around the coffee machine contributes to increased productivity?"

Actually, yes, it does. But there's no point trying to convince anybody of that. That would be like trying to convince someone that the earth is round. It is. Take it or leave it. Nevertheless, I still find it exasperating when a manager fails to recognise the importance of horizontal communication, especially the significant role of relationships.

The relationship factor

Relationship is the opposite of isolation. When individuals engage in horizontal communication they build a relationship that goes beyond the immediate task-related objective. Since the fiasco with the lab explosion, Andrea and Stewart have been on good terms and chat frequently about this and that, including new developments in Birmingham and London. Recently, Stewart made a pretty big mistake at work. Guess what happened?

Andrea stepped in and took over his work package that he hadn't completed yet without a cross word to him. I asked her:

"Would you have helped Stewart out like that five months ago?"

"No way! Back then I thought he was an arrogant so and so."

"Why did you change your mind?"

"Well, we got to know each other a little better, and I realised he's really quite ok."

"Would you let Zoe in Stockholm get away with what Stewart got away with?"

"I don't think so. I don't get on with her very well."

"Really? What makes you say that?"

"Well, I suppose we've not really had much opportunity to get to know each other, now you mention it. Hell, if that's really the cause, why doesn't someone do something about it? Isn't that Bill's job? And what about our steering committee? Does it actually provide us with guidance or is 'steering' just a name?"

Good questions. It took me five minutes to explain to Andrea that while she understands that leading virtual teams involves more than meets the eye, it's largely unexplored terrain to outsiders.

> Horizontal communication creates rapport. Team members who share rapport are much more productive than individuals who communicate about the task in hand and ignore the relationship factor.

In other words:

> If you could put together a team in which the members sustain a workable relationship, why would you hesitate?

Or, in more pragmatic terms:

> Count on the strength of the relationship among team members!

Why is it that every manager understands that in theory, but so few of them put it into practice? Because the significance of informal, horizontal communication is vastly underestimated when it comes to virtual team leadership and overcoming virtual isolation. Don't make the same mistake.

Another reason is that managers are often not overly talkative in general and can be sparse with their communication within the team. While many subscribe to the adage: "Leadership is 90% communication," they rarely practise it. They tend to communicate about the job in hand and leave it at that. In conventional teams, the more aware members compensate for this weakness in leadership by sharing off the record. Virtual teams don't have the opportunity to do this simply because they are separated by distance. That gives rise to a peculiar little paradox:

You won't reach your goals in virtual teams if communication
within your team is just about the task.

If you want to achieve excellence in your virtual team, then your team
members need to communicate so well informally and horizontally that
they create a healthy team spirit. How do you create that kind of team
spirit? There are many ways. Which way is best? You've guessed it: it
begins with K.

K as in kick-off

The kick-off event is a classic exercise in futility. What happens when a
project leader finally convinces top management of the absolute necessity of a kick-off to launch a large-scale new project?

That's right. A number of different senior managers give long-winded
presentations complete with PowerPoint monologues on how important
the project is for the company and how they expect it to be handled.
That entire scenario is embarrassingly ineffective:

Personal relationships, managing isolation and team spirit
are not going to happen while sitting and listening to a
presentation for hours on end!

So how do you create personal relationships? I'm astonished that I am
still asked this question. Imagine, a well-paid individual asks me how to
go about creating personal relationships. As if civilisation were 4 years
old, not 40,000. You already have the answer. It's as simple as this:

Personal relationships develop through interaction.

If some unteachable manager wants to call that having a 'chit chat' then that's fine with me – it's among the most effective measures for boosting communication. During one of these two-hour 'chats' within the scope of a kick-off, for example, it turned out that the project designer had won a junior world-cup downhill race. From then on, his nickname was 'The Champion'. Every time 'The Champion' called or sent an email, the recipient announced to his office mates: "Hey, listen to what The Champion has to say!" Anyone who's worked in a place where work really happens knows how important this kind of kidding around with each other is for team performance. Good-natured teasing is a sign that individuals feel comfortable with each other and are likely to support one another when the going gets tough. By the end of the kick-off, every member had a nickname. Upon reaching the first milestone, the team leader distributed Manchester United T-shirts to each member with his/her nickname written on the back.

Who wouldn't forfeit a month's pay to work in that kind of team? Who would be so naive as to believe that in a team like that the productivity curve *wouldn't* skyrocket?

So what's the key?

Benefit of the doubt and other herd instinct phenomena

What causes the most inefficiencies in project teams? Think about it. What do your years of experience and your competence tell you?

Even conventional teams experience rampant inefficiency
from time to time due to disagreement, misunderstanding
and lack of communication.

If your only contact with someone is through email, you're much more likely to read things between the lines that may not even be there. As you know, this tendency is directly proportional to the quality of the relationship.

Similarly, we're much more likely to interpret the intentions of our managers in a more negative light than is the case with a colleague. That's not necessarily because we like the colleague better. It is because our relationships with colleagues are often stronger.

If you don't know the person on the receiving end of your
phone calls or emails personally, you risk getting entangled
in unnecessary misunderstandings.

Misunderstandings that could easily be avoided. For example, a kick-off event where team members chat informally and share experiences without a top-level manager standing by looking cross. Why do they do that? Because of a simple absurdity.

Many top managers shy away from too much personal contact because they pay no heed to the soft skill factor. The reason is often enough a bruised ego: "Not on my time! Their job is to listen to me and not to talk to *each other*! There's enough time to talk later at the bar if they really have to. We're strictly here for business and not small talk." Oh dear.

Personal interaction not only prevents the usual misunderstandings that can arise within a team. It also defuses much of the conflict potential in projects. If someone I don't know crosses me, I'll wait for payback time. If, however, 'The Champion' occasionally oversteps the mark, I'll be less likely to hold it against him. And why should I? He's our champ after all – he didn't really mean to say that! He's just having a bad day, that's all. We all know what that's like:

> **Good relationships enhance good will.**

Ok, message understood. Team members sharing information informally and horizontally impacts overall performance. But just how does this impact performance? Nice to have? Or is it integral to success? Here's an interesting analogy:

> **Communication within the team is like an iceberg: one-seventh of the project's success is due to factual communication. Personal communication comprises six-sevenths.**

That's incredible! And it explains why even well-equipped virtual teams with renowned experts on board so often fail to deliver: communication acts like an iceberg. The one-seventh of task content emerges out of the water and is visible; the other, predominant six-sevenths, or the personal and relationship factors, remain below the surface. They will inevitably sink the Titanic if they aren't recognised in time. When two icebergs collide they crash below the surface. That's dramatic and can prove embarrassing. Quite spontaneously, the question arises: are we dependent on the leadership of captains who don't know the first thing about icebergs? Wow, what are they doing at the helm? And what are they being paid for, for heaven's sake?

A question to ask yourself: do you lead your team on the surface level or are you the kind of leader who looks below the surface?

What does all this mean? How do you establish horizontal communication in your team and avoid isolation? Let's take a closer look at how that can work with the help of two checklists: the first for the team leader and the second for the team members.

Checklist: horizontal communication for team leaders

☑ Isolation is the enemy of productivity in virtual teams.

☑ Horizontal communication is the enemy of isolation.

☑ A kick-off event is the best way for team members to get to know each other and create sustainable working relationships.

☑ Is your project already underway? No problem. Do it now! Better late than never, or as American therapist Tad James would say: "It's never too late for a happy childhood!" That goes for teams as well.

☑ A kick-off includes setting goals and task information, of course. Task information in itself, however, doesn't prevent isolation. Knowing how the other person communicates is more important than facts alone in order to avoid unnecessary misunderstandings later on.

☑ Be sure to make a place in the agenda for systematic and moderated icebreaker rounds for team members to mingle and get to know each other on a personal level (get the agreement of those senior managers who are present). It builds trust, and trust is the opposite of isolation.

☑ Go a little beyond the usual round of introductions by gathering personal information such as: what is the team member's role in the company? His/her experience on previous projects? Where do the priorities lie in their work? What are their likes and dislikes? Hobbies? What kind of music do they like? Favourite books or films?

☑ Encourage the team members to engage in horizontal communication. It often seems like people have simply forgotten how to engage in conversation from one human being to another. Be patient and stick with it! The first ice-breaker moments are the most difficult.

☑ Introduce a feedback system for the ongoing project: who gives whom feedback about what and in what way? Who is informed when and by whom about deviations from the project plan? The feedback system is an important tool for conventional teams. Its significance for virtual teams is dramatic.

☑ Agree on guidelines for giving feedback. For example, it should be short and to the point. Always about behaviour, never personal. Always timely and clear. Separate the person from the behaviour. Feedback should only be given face-to-face. Remember the 3 steps of successful feedback: first, your specific observation. Then the impact it has on you. Then your wish or request for the future. This is especially important for virtual teams. Better once too often than not enough. And small talk (in acceptable doses) is ok and indeed desirable!

☑ Encourage team spirit and walk your talk! Acknowledge good work where appropriate! Don't be miserly with praise!

☑ When you send team members from different locations to training courses (which happens frequently in virtual teams), instead of offering training seminars locally, e.g. members from the Coventry office first, then from the Newcastle office and so on, use the occasion to bring members together for networking, establishing rapport and engaging in horizontal communication.

Checklist: horizontal communication for team members

☑ Team spirit is not solely the team leader's privilege! If you appreciate a good team atmosphere, do what you can!

☑ If, for example, you think that a colleague did a great job, let him and all the others know. Write an email to everyone. Praise the others' productivity.

☑ When there's trouble on the other hand, the rule is: don't copy people on cc! Trouble should be addressed face-to-face or on the phone. Addressing conflict in front of the entire team is sometimes tempting and understandable, but it's bound to do more harm than good.

☑ Just in case you're the shy type: start small. An email with a comment about the weather where you are or something similar (stress at work or special events) is pretty standard these days.

☑ Don't be afraid to write about more than task communication and give your emails or phone calls a personal note at the beginning and end. Loosen up a little with colleagues on your team and get to know them a little better.

☑ Recognise your colleagues' communication patterns and make an effort to adapt: does he/she communicate more succinctly? Does he/she prefer a more personal touch? Does he/she appreciate praise? Does he/she enjoy "a bit of a moan about the management"?

☑ Allow time for personal interaction, even if you're in a hurry. Personal moments like that are valuable investments in team spirit. In appropriate doses they are more important than the current task at hand.

☑ As with most things in life: 'temperance is the key' is good advice! A total lack of personal contact is as damaging as hours of 'chit chat'.

☑ If a colleague offends you, stay calm and don't give way to a spontaneous reaction. It's better to take a deep breath, a step back and ask how the comment was meant.

☑ Don't confront colleagues with remarks such as: "I'm sick and tired of your bossy tone!" You may have a point, but accusations have a way of escalating. Try giving effective feedback by mentioning how a particular comment upsets you. For example: "When I read 'immediately', I felt like I had a gun pointed at my head. I'm sure you didn't mean it like that." Most people aren't stupid; they may just lack empathy.

☑ Practise the age old legal adage, *in dubio pro reo* or 'innocent until proven guilty'. Give your colleague the benefit of the doubt. You are team-mates after all. Believe that your colleague means well until proven otherwise.

Liberate your team!

What's your perspective? Be selfish for a moment. Ask yourself: what does my dream team look like? In which kind of team would I perform best? Would that be a team in which members don't know each other, and communication is limited to the task at hand both in emails and over the phone? Where mistrust poisons the team spirit, each member suspecting the other of having some sort of intrigue up their sleeve? Where each member looks out for number one? Where people spend hours or days splitting hairs and documenting minute details to prove innocence just in case push comes to shove, instead of bringing the project forward?

The fact that you're reading this page shows that you're not interested in working in a toxic team like the one described above (sociopaths don't bother with this book). Of course, many of us work in companies and departments where a culture of mistrust prevails. That means:

> Consciously breaking with the predominant company or departmental culture in order to create a productive team culture. Just do it!

That's not to say that the predominant culture is malignant. All it takes is a culture that propagates expert competence as the deciding factor in projects. That's a doubtful approach even in conventional projects. In virtual teams it defies better judgement.

> Virtual team success means breaking out of isolation through subject competence, project competence and team competence, and by being a competent freedom fighter.

You don't believe you can be all those things? That's what many project leaders believe. One comment I heard once was: "I'm an engineer. I have enough problems with the eternal small talk at official gatherings! Now you want me to help create an informal communication culture within the team!" A lot of people feel that way but it's not normally true.

Even engineers and other highly specialised experts can be seen conversing easily with particular individuals under particular circumstances about topics that have nothing to do with work. There is no such thing as the purely one-dimensional expert!

> The trick is: catch yourself in situations where you are demonstrating competence in horizontal communication without thinking about it and benchmark yourself.
> Now transfer this new skill to the team context.

After realising the benefits of the approach, this same engineer said: "Actually, there's nothing to it: if I can do it in situation x, I should be able to do the same in situation y ... right?" Okay, that's thinking like a typical engineer. But that's exactly right. If you want to give the beast a name, call it the Bright Spot Approach: transfer your skill from the exception (bright spot) to the rule. It's worth it!

It's worth it

Take radioactivity for example: you can't see it, smell it or touch it. But it's still effective. It's the same with isolation in virtual teams. It's invisible, but extremely virulent. Putting this complex concept into a nutshell, one could say:

> Isolated teams underperform. Liberated teams do well.

Now, you know how to free up your team. It's neither difficult nor complex, but not easy. You're up against the "near impenetrable wall of ignorance in the world", as I was once told by a project leader in an especially 'financially efficient' company. It takes both courage and a strong will. The good news is: good project leaders and managers as well as competent team members benefit considerably. It's well worth the effort.

Liberated teams not only perform better and ultimately contribute to your success, it's also a joy to be part of such a team. I often hear comments such as: "I can hardly wait for the next team telco. I really enjoy sharing views with a good group of people and moving a worthwhile project forward. It's not really possible in our department." That's the reward liberation brings.

In brief: Escape from isolation!

- As a rule, virtual team members are isolated from each other.
- Liberate yourself from this imposed isolation!
- Liberation is not just nice to have. It's a key factor for virtual team success.
- The better the informal, horizontal communication in the team, the better the team will perform.
- The ideal place to start is the kick-off event.
- It's never too late to make up for a lack of a kick-off!
- At the heart of horizontal communication is personal interaction on topics besides the project work.
- Leave room for team members to share personal experiences, approaches to work, likes and dislikes at work and the way communication takes place in the team. These parameters play a decisive role in horizontal communication.
- Agree on rules for giving feedback and practice them in role-play. Most people *understand* the concept of feedback but due to lack of practice, only a few really *master* the art.
- Enrich the content information you send to team members by email or tell them on the phone with one or two sentences that have a personal touch. With practice, this comes automatically and lubricates the team engine.
- You can skip all technical advice on how to cultivate personal interaction in your team if you and other members of your team take a sincere, authentic interest in each other.

Sounds crazy doesn't it? Sincere interest other people seems to have fallen by the wayside in modern civilisation. That explains the attractiveness and outstanding success of liberated virtual teams: life is better there and it's open to all of us!

> "One single person can transform a family dynamic, a
> team and a company - provided there's a will."
>
> Jeri W., team manager

5. Form your team!

||||||||||||||||||||||||||||||||||||||||||||||||||||||||||

Is that really necessary?

You are assigned the position of project manager. What's the first thing you think of?

Obviously, you think first about the project, the outcome and the tight time schedule. What don't you think of?

Correct: you don't think about the team. Not immediately anyway. If indeed you get around to it, it's with a rather nagging feeling, or to put it more precisely, with a feeling of cognitive dissonance:

> We know we've got to form the team, but who's got the
> time? The motivation? The know-how? And the courage?

We're well aware of the fact that teams have to be formed. Many of us learned this in a training course entitled 'team development' that every leader and (hopefully) every higher-level project manager is obliged to attend. That's where we get to know the four phases of team development:

1) Forming: getting acquainted (like on the first date).
2) Storming: there's trouble brewing (when the honeymoon is over).
3) Norming: the team agrees on common guidelines.
4) Performing: the team moves towards high performance.

Do I detect a raised eyebrow or a sardonic grin here? True, these four phases tend to be neglected on a regular basis in conventional teams. Even more so in virtual teams. Team leaders often ask me:

- "Does there have to be a forming phase? Even for virtual teams?"
- "We're all located at different sites and can't meet up. Which means we do without!"
- "We've set up virtual teams in order to save costs and get the job done faster. It makes little sense to invest extra time and money to form the team!"

As one managing director explained to me: "I don't pay people to travel all the way here just to get to know each other! I don't run a travel agency and, for that matter, not a dating agency either!" Another senior manager asked: "How can we replace forming?" To answer that question, let's take a look at what happens without professional team development. From an empirical standpoint that's quite simple.

Most conventional teams start off without any kind of formal forming and storming. They just do it informally. And where does that happen? That's right. Around the water cooler, of course, and at other informal events. That's where the team gets together informally to fill in the gaps that leadership failed to address. It's where they really get to know each other on a personal level and, while they're at it, resolve their first conflicts. Now just imagine a virtual team. What do you think is bound to happen?

Here too, the answer is simple: due to the distance, they never get past the forming phase. As a result, they carry out their conflicts just below the surface. And they fight like cats and dogs! Like anyone would if they were thrown together haphazardly into a workgroup. But the leadership team has no idea this is happening because team members settle things among themselves by resorting to hidden conflict. These are the worst kinds of conflicts, because what lies hidden can't be addressed. You can't manage what you can't see! It's hard to believe: management resides in a sort of protective cocoon, and when the shell they've created comes crashing in around them because the hidden conflicts surface, they fall back on the old management myth: "Virtual teams just have more conflicts than normal teams!" That's absolute nonsense. They have just as many as conventional teams; however they are only recognised much later. That's one scenario.

The other is: open or hidden conflict doesn't develop in the virtual team. Instead, it bubbles beneath the surface as latent antipathy like a smouldering volcano. This is one of the most effective ways to kill efficiency. And still managers ask if forming is necessary? Think again!

What must be done

Is forming a must? That depends on what you want. If all you need is a work group rather than a team, that performs routine tasks without team spirit or expectations of excellence, then doing without forming is not likely to make a difference. Although it would of course be helpful.

However, as soon as you find yourself facing a challenge for which you need the help of a high-performance (virtual) team in order to reach demanding goals the motto is:

There is no substitute for forming!

It's no great issue if a conventional team skips the forming phase in the beginning. It can always be formed along the way, even at a later date. In fact, you don't have to get involved. People tend to sense how much better it is to work with people they know better and will find ways to meet informally by any of the means already discussed ad nauseum in the preceding chapters. It's common sense for members of conventional teams to seek out opportunities to get to know each other informally. In fact, it has become such a commonplace practice that it's become known as the 'water cooler moment'.

In many English-speaking countries a water cooler on every floor of an office building is a common sight. To get a break from the dry office air, employees meet regularly around the water cooler to get a drink and chat informally. This intermittent break from office routine has, over time, become a ritual, ergo: 'the water cooler moment'. Heads of department or team leaders may have no idea about team forming. A conventional team, however, will easily make up for this oversight around the water cooler. Virtual teams don't benefit from this kind of corrective action inspired by collective human common sense. At least not as long as there are no project-specific online water coolers available.

Clearly, virtual teams are so far removed from each other and hence isolated that it is difficult to get to know one another personally. As obvious as that sounds, it has dire consequences:

> **Unformed virtual teams create problems that are rarely recognised as typical team-forming problems.**

All you notice is that something is going wrong, but you're not aware of what's causing it. You're not aware that underneath the task-related issue (visible), the conflict (visible), or the tangible antagonism within the team (visible), there lies a forming problem (not visible). Quite often this obliviousness is given the wrong label: "That's just how virtual teams work!" That's not true: it's just how *unformed* teams work!

That's one reason I have no qualms about emphasising my earlier advice (see chapter 4): invest in a kick-off event! It's the best investment you can make at the start of a project. And it's not just about forming the team or for team members to get acquainted and begin creating the all-important team spirit – it's also about risk prevention.

Virtual risk management

In chapters 1-3 we talked extensively about the risks that virtual teams face: great distances and resulting isolation, lack of informal and horizontal communication, the danger to team spirit, misunderstandings, conflict, and losses due to friction and resulting inefficiency. As a team leader you're certainly familiar with these risks. Don't you think your team members should be too?

> Increase your team's sensitivity to the dangers of virtual work. That way you're not alone in dealing with the risks. Virtual team leadership is also teamwork: everyone can and should support the effort.

Calling the team members' attention to and theorising about the dangers of virtual communication is not enough. Agree on appropriate countermeasures: personal relationships among team members, horizontal communication and feedback rules. Emphasise the importance of dealing with each other constructively, build and sustain trust, gain votes of confidence from decision-makers, and learn to tolerate ambiguity. As already mentioned, the best framework for these agreements is the forming phase. That's why a smart virtual team leader will never ask: "Is there a way we can replace the forming phase?" Instead he will ask: "What's the best way to form a virtual team?"

The partial answer to this question is: it's best done at the kick-off event. This comment often causes team leaders to frown in consternation: "Don't tell me! Tell my boss! He's the one who has to approve the budget." That's absolutely right.

Please regard the line of reasoning in support of a kick-off as a support, not a reproach. See it as a series of arguments that will help you convince your management of the necessity for and benefits of a kick-off. What do you think your chances are? I'd say they're pretty good.

Speaking from experience, I can say that team leaders who complain about the unreasonableness of their management rarely get their kick-off approved (complainers don't change things). Team leaders who assume their chances of getting approval for a kick-off are hopeless anyway don't usually succeed in getting a kick-off. Those team leaders who do get approval for a kick-off have usually fought hard for it.

> A good team leader doesn't give up when he meets resistance to an idea he finds worthwhile.

There is a question I'm frequently asked by project leaders who have long since realised the benefits of a kick-off: what does it take to enlighten the eternal sceptics and bean counters? This question is often asked by project managers who have recognised the need for a kick-off but are up against the resistance of procurement departments and steering committees. They ask what the best arguments are for getting budget approval quickly and easily. Here are a handful of the best.

Persuasive arguments for a kick-off

☑ Nothing impresses bean counters more than figures. So give them what they want. Say, for example: "My team consists of twelve members. If they don't get to know each other before work starts, there's bound to be friction, misunderstanding, start-up difficulties and conflict along the way. If each team member loses just fifteen minutes a day this way, it adds up to 75 minutes per week, which multiplied by 12 members adds up to 15 hours wasted unnecessarily week after week. Our project will run for X weeks, multiplied by 15 hours a week times the calculated hourly wage equals Y euros. Now compare that to the investment in a workshop plus the working hours that a kick-off will cost. Clearly, the kick-off is much less expensive!"

☑ Second argument: transparency. Another strong stance, for example, might be, "We need to determine from the start and once and for all who will be reporting to whom, when and how, and which information will be shared and documented. That can't be done by an order from the top. It's only possible in an actual meeting where these issues can be discussed, coordinated and agreed upon. A lack of transparency causes confusion; confusion impedes processes, and impeded processes add up to inefficiency, increased costs and slowing down the project unnecessarily!"

☑ A simple argument: A kick-off increases team motivation and motivation is something that doesn't come with a price tag.

☑ "Compare the ratio of projects that reached their goals, both with and without an initial kick-off," provided, of course, you have estimates or comparative figures to refer to (why else do we have our Controllers?). If you do you can say: "Projects initiated with a kick-off event are much less likely to fall behind schedule on delivery times and exceed the budget. Moreover, they are more on target with their performance goals. In short, you save money!"

☑ Ergo: a kick-off is not a cost factor. On the contrary, it's an investment with a considerable return.

Why not try out these arguments the next time you find yourself dealing with a hard-core number-cruncher! Your best bet to get things moving faster and avoid persuasive argumentation is if you can manage to get a senior decision-maker to join the kick-off. That convinces very well. Provided the kick-off is well planned and moderated.

Forming: Getting the team in shape

I've occasionally come across top decision-makers who join the kick-off with a "What's this psychobabble all about?" mindset and walk out with a feeling of enthusiasm in the end: "Wow, what was that? That was amazing! The team spirit was almost palpable!" That's not unusual for a professionally managed kick-off event. What's the reason?

Why does forming have such an impact on teams? Well, it's a result of the imparity principle inherent in interpersonal perception:

> People who don't know each other tend to perceive the differences between each other first. People who know each other perceive their commonalities first.

The idea is so banal that even the Rolling Stones caught on to it as Mick Jagger croons in 'Satisfaction': "He can't be a man 'cause he doesn't smoke the same cigarettes as me." Differences separate humans; when something appears unfamiliar, most people and practically all stressed-out managers will perceive the differences first. That's a phenomenon that has nothing to do with xenophobia. It goes back to a 40,000-year-old survival instinct: is the stranger I've just met carrying a battle-axe and I'm not? Differences could be fatal back then. It's different now of course. However, 40,000 years count for no more than a split second as far as our genomes are concerned. That's not enough time for our genes to change.

It's a shame that this knowledge about our Neanderthal ancestry has yet to reach the echelons of management. Otherwise, every manager would have to cry out in dismay: "… and we force individuals with this primal instinct into virtual teams without further thought on the matter? We're risking blood and thunder!" Do you see? All because of perceived differences. That's the secret behind forming.

> The forming secret: the more individuals get to know each other, the less they focus on differences, and the more they focus on commonalities. Discovery of commonalities is the motor that drives team spirit.

This dynamic develops after the first 20 to 30 minutes and grows stronger by the hour. After a day spent together, the effect takes shape and becomes sustainable.

> The secret behind forming is developing trust based on the discovery of commonalities.

Ok, so what? So you discover a few commonalities. What's so great about that? Everything! Because the commonalities you discover activate another, age-old and therefore extremely powerful instinct, namely: affection. This is best expressed by the saying:

People who are like each other, like each other.

Affection for another person is not merely a touchy-feely thing. It's a well-defined recipe for success. It's not about blonde hair or good manners, it's about commonalities. If I come across someone who is similar to me (or, as Jagger puts it, who smokes the same brand of cigarettes, for example), I'll like and trust him instinctively even before my cerebral cortex can tell me anything about him.

It's the commonalities that keep the team together and create identity. Five minutes is not enough for a team to discover commonalities, nor will it happen if they are dispersed around the globe or limit conversations to the task at hand. It takes time, proximity and the chance to get to know one another personally.

Commonalities create affection, trust and team spirit.

I often wonder about managers who go on about 'team spirit', and in the same breath refer to forming as 'psychobabble' or refuse to cough up a budget for a kick-off. I wouldn't risk that for fear that every junior trainee would notice how little I know about team spirit.

Team spirit can't be forced, only encouraged.

The best way to ignite team spirit is to start in the forming phase. Forming gives virtual teams the opportunity to discover similarities.

It is a misconception that commonalities can be professed
in words only, or can they be invoked at will such as in:
"We have so much in common!" Commonalities need to be
discovered. Together.

That takes time, but not that much. A kick-off is time enough. You need
to take the time if you want a team with real team spirit. Why should
you be satisfied with less? Why should you be the one who doesn't deserve the team with team spirit? Why make life more difficult for yourself
and your team? Why should you be responsible for a project where the
team goes to work with the handbrake on?

The answer to these questions is simple: because an awful lot of practi-
tioners have no idea how to discover commonalities. Have you ever been
to an afternoon tea dance?

The tea dance syndrome

In today's industrialised world we have forgotten the simplest human practices. Many of us behave like a country mouse who attends
an afternoon tea dance in the big city only to stand in the corner
because he/she never learnt how to make contact. I've experienced
project managers with academic backgrounds or backgrounds in the
natural sciences trying desperately to start up a conversation much
to the embarrassment of all involved in the team meeting, especially
of the team leader. Even though discovering commonalities is not
rocket science. Believe me:

Just let the people take turns to talk about their areas of
responsibility in the company, their interests, preferences
and dislikes about their work and ways of communicating;
their expectations and concerns regarding the project.
Encourage questions and comments. Emphasise
commonalities such as: "So you studied in London too?
So did Karen and I! When did you graduate?"

If people are reluctant to engage in conversation, then use a flipchart: 1)
name, 2) area of responsibility in the company, 3) area of specialisation,
4) ... then all participants go through the points out loud. That helps in
overcoming the 'country mouse' shyness.

It also helps to allow for generous coffee breaks. People are naturally
curious about each other and like to talk about themselves. So loosen
up and forget your resistance to introductory rounds. Even if you don't
know how to proceed in the beginning, don't worry, people will work it
out with a little gentle nudging. It can't go wrong if you relax about it and
take over the facilitation.

Showing a sincere interest in your team members is a
great help.

Some examples of this kind would be: "Really? This is the third project
of this kind that you've worked on? I am glad we have an expert like
you on board. Does anyone else have a similar experience? Positive or
not so positive?" Bingo! You're in the hub of the discussion, interacting with and getting to know your teammates. By the way, you're no
doubt familiar with these kinds of conversations. You have them with
friends, colleagues and family members. Just bring such informal ex-

changes into forming. Is that all there is to it? Yes, it's that easy when you know how to do it.

High-performance teams keep doing it

What makes a high-performance team? It's a strange question because it is so rarely asked. Somehow I can't manage to rid myself of the impression that project management seems to revolve entirely around the project while ignoring the team. I'm not referring to you here, of course. After all, you've chosen to read a book about what makes high-performance teams, which puts you in the ranks of the intellectual elite of project management. You deserve to discover the secret:

> **High-performance teams don't stop at the kick-off.**
> **They bring in forming elements on a regular basis.**

That's one reason (aside from the task) why high-performance teams on larger and longer-term projects hold regular face-to-face meetings. Not all members are obliged to attend at every meeting. What counts is that enough time is planned in for sharing informally to strengthen the common bond in addition to discussing project updates. It sounds logical: once is not enough. No social construction can thrive without regular, careful maintenance. That goes for families, sports teams, clubs, departments: no team, no marriage (although many couples are trying out the low-maintenance version, hence the high divorce rate). Team spirit is not perpetual.

> **Team spirit requires maintenance.**

In order to thrive, team spirit needs to be recharged on a regular basis through personal interaction between individuals. I'm pretty sure the technocrats would love to do away with the notion that it's vital for a team's success. As long as people are part of the business world, however, the human touch is indispensable. Everyone is free to ignore this fact at his/her own risk.

You say your hands are tied? Regular get-togethers are not possible for whatever reasons? Well, that can happen. What does that mean for you?

Virtual forming

I'll let you in on another secret: management is not about management: it's about character.

When it's impossible to schedule regular face-to-face meetings, many team leaders throw in the towel and skip the forming phase of the project. "What's the use anyway?" That's the easy way out. Team leaders with a stronger character say, "Now more than ever!" That's the right attitude.

> The more impossible regular in-person meetings are, the more important virtual forming measures become to the survival and success of the team.

There are many ways to form a virtual team. Let your creativity run wild. For example, you could set up a project website on the intranet or a virtual wall of fame with pictures and personal profiles of team members. You can join project forums that encourage discussion and sharing opinions. One such project group in the media branch, for instance, has its own virtual 'project gazette'. All team members contribute to its content, and it's distributed daily via email. Which possibilities can you think of?

If this sounds a bit childish to you, you're absolutely right. It's totally childish! Just recently I was called to intervene in a virtual team where R&D and Production Control had crossed swords to the point that they were two weeks behind the first milestone! First, I met with the head of R&D of the team in Munich who said: "Those slowcoaches in Production at the Romanian plant are sabotaging the entire project!" I didn't counter. Instead I casually pulled out a few photographs: "Oh, you mean those slowcoaches?" I showed him some family photos of the three members of the Romanian production control team. He had never even seen his colleagues.

He had merely spoken to them over the phone and corresponded via email. After he had seen the photos, the derogatory term 'slowcoach' was dropped from his vocabulary. Benefit of the doubt is an early step in the development of team spirit. A few photos can make the difference? That's childish. And extremely effective. If team spirit is 'childish' then, please, I'd like to be the most childish team leader around.

Admittedly, a virtual get-together will never replace physical presence. However, if your people can't meet in person then they'll have to improvise the forming process.

It goes without saying that top teams use virtual forming to augment the face-to-face kick-off event instead of as a substitute. They exercise as many options as possible to open the way for informal interaction among members to facilitate forming. Regardless of how you go about integrating virtual forming: just do it and trust that it will work!

That reminds me of a remarkable example from the field.

Swapping recipes

A French team leader was tasked with developing a new after-sales ser-
vice on a shoestring budget; shoestring meaning no budget for a kick-
off, face-to-face forming and other necessary measures. Luckily for her,
she had a skilled programmer on board who designed a virtual pin-
board for her. Each team member posted a picture of him/herself (with
or without family). A brief synopsis of competencies; project experience,
as well as likes and dislikes and hobbies. Attached to the pin board is
a forum where, just hours after posting, the first team members from
different countries had begun sharing cooking recipes. The British and
Germans discussed the newly acquired players at Manchester United
and Bayern Munich and all of them together placed bets on the outcome
of an ongoing international sports event. What do you think the boss's
reaction was to all that?

That's right. The boss complained: "What do they think they're doing
swapping bloody recipes? They're supposed to be working!" A year later
the team delivered great results, whereupon the boss said: "See? It pays
to focus on work instead of swapping recipes!" What was the project
leader's response? Nothing, to him at least. To her team she said: "Some
people will never get it." Two or three project successes like that and she
will be in a position where her word will have more clout than her in-
corrigible boss. That will change the company culture. One person can
change the world.

Top results with the help of recipes? That's right. It's the fine art of virtual team leadership. That's why you'll hardly be surprised if our next tool
for virtual forming under discussion is the chat room.

Let them chat!

Be very sure to create a project chat room. The good people in your team will interact informally by email anyway. Offer this option of virtual forming to encourage everybody to engage in interaction and to form the team. The nice side effect is you can see the chat going on and there are fewer rumours behind your back. Just don't play the watchdog. That destroys forming.

Of course, you can expect the resistance of the die-hard stick-in-the-muds: "The team isn't here to chat, they're here to get the job done!" In the age of the Internet such atavistic thinking is way out of line as any school kid will attest to. But there are too few school kids in management, so prepare yourself for the flack and ignore it as much as possible. Say: "Absolutely!" And continue your chat. You could also try management from the bottom up and coach the stick-in-the-muds: "Our team members are only able to do a good job if they have the chance to interact informally. It builds team spirit and is a professionally acknowledged tool for forming teams." Try it. You might get through to them.

One smart project leader once referred to the chat room as the virtual team's virtual 'water cooler'. That's exactly what it is. And, as we all know, that's where the best ideas are generated, especially for projects. Why should you do without the best ideas only because someone doesn't get the point?

How do we talk to each other?

It doesn't matter whether this belongs to forming or norming. It is so important and so often forgotten:

> Agree on a few rules during Forming, including some basic communication rules. Rules help in Forming and Norming a team.

For example, agree that emails are to be answered within 24 or 48 hours, at least with confirmation of receipt, including a 'Thank You' of course. Let the sender know when he/she can expect a full reply.

> Talk about how you want to talk to each other in the team!

A team without such agreements, in which everyone squabbles amongst themselves, will never be a high-performance team. It goes without saying that real team leaders adhere to these communication rules during all interaction in the team. If need be, he/she will step in with a firm and friendly reminder to stick to the rules. Sometimes the things that form the team are quite simple. That is simple but not necessarily easy.

A virtual weekly team meeting

Every well-managed department has a weekly team meeting. Provided it doesn't turn into the department head's one-man show, it serves to drive productivity. The same is true for virtual teams:

> The weekly team meeting for virtual teams can be held as a telephone or video conference.

Naturally, you'll be discussing factual information, milestone status, work packages, use of resources, reaching goals and next steps. That's a must. After the main points have been discussed, the fine art of virtual leadership sets in and continues the forming process.

Old-school project leaders might occasionally pick up on the emotional temperature of the team while discussing the project's nuts and bolts: "I wonder why there's a strange mood in the team today?" and continue the task-focused course without further thought. The more competent team members regroup around the water cooler to repair the de-forming damage caused. A professional team leader, on the other hand, senses the team's mood and addresses it: "Ok guys, I have the impression that there's something in the air here. Can we talk about it?" The responses that come up then have to be carefully listened to and answered. Many members experience a veritable eureka moment:

> **A virtual team leader needs considerably more social and communication competence than a 'regular' project manager if he/she wants to be successful.**

It takes time and nerves of course, to take people's feelings and moods into consideration. You also need a way with words (in brief: leadership competence). *Not* paying attention to the team's emotional temperature will cost you even more time and nerves! If people build up animosities one day, they'll begin sabotaging each other the next. Those who are new to the task find it difficult to manage moods and emotions. The seasoned project leader doesn't wait until the team's mood gets hopelessly bogged down. Instead he senses discord and addresses it before it becomes toxic.

Regular reflection

When the mood in the team threatens to stall productivity it's already too late. It's better to test the waters *before* the damage is done. Real virtual leaders manage to include phases of reflection during the weekly team meeting, in face-to-face meetings, in telephone and video conferences and in the chat room. This sounds like a big deal, but it's fairly standard.

Professional team leaders ask regularly: "Let's leave project scheduling and our tasks aside for the moment. Let's take a minute to talk about our team. What is going well and what's making our collaboration work? What should we definitely keep and what needs to be changed?"

> Regular reflection avoids upset.

There's no need to have the team reflect for any great length of time. Five to twenty minutes is plenty depending on the need to talk. The going might be a bit tough at the beginning, especially if team members are not used to being asked about how they are feeling and other important issues by their boss. Be patient. The hesitation will pass with time.

The better your communication skills, the easier this is. What do I mean by communication skills? Here's a brief example:

- "Oh c'mon, why get upset if the Spaniards insist on dawdling?" That is poor communication. The team member who voiced this concern is likely to avoid reflection in future. By trivialising the team member's concern, the team leader shows he doesn't take it seriously. A probably unintentional denigration of the team member's comment. Communication competence in action could sound like this: "You'd like the Spaniards to respond to your questions more promptly? I can understand that. How quickly would you like them to respond? And how is that for you, dear Spaniard?"

I agree, that's not easy. During the normal workday we often talk without giving much thought to what we're really communicating. But that's exactly the difference between successful and less successful team managers. A competent team manager thinks first before he speaks. He speaks with forming in mind. Why is this so rare in daily practice? Because fear inhibits.

Fear of conflict

Every halfway sensible person understands that the better the mood in the team, the better the productivity, and that the mood gets better the more you address it and care about it: "So how are people feeling? What's working? What isn't?" These are three simple questions that create a panicked reaction for 90 per cent of all people within and outside of the corporate world. Why?

That's right. I'm sure you've already worked it out. Because anyone who asks these three questions risks the shit hitting the fan and being splattered with accusations, damnation, complaints, criticism, emotional outbursts, and an orgy of justifications. Three words say it all: ultimate conflict potential! Experienced professionals don't mince words here: "There's no way I'm going to ask them how they feel! They'll moan at me no end!" This does seem somewhat absurd:

> People prefer to sacrifice 30 to 70 percent of team performance rather than listen to their team's concerns for 10 minutes.

Don't be soft. Could that be you? No, I don't think so. You're still reading this book after all. Wimps don't read books about forming virtual teams. Virtual leaders aren't wimps. Why not? Because they know:

- The more time people have to voice their concerns and get them out of their system the better. A lot of teams have built up issues over time that can drastically hamper team performance.
- The earlier you begin with rounds of reflection, the lower the build-up of team frustrations! Declare simply: "Ok, now we're going to do some straight talking! But there'll be no personal attacks! Read my lips: no accusations, no blaming!"
- People can communicate without accusing or blaming, for instance, using I-messages or the sandwich technique for giving feedback. If you need to, remind them to do so in a friendly but firm way. Even Schwarzenegger and van Damme are afraid of conflict. But they confront it anyway. Because they know that if you avoid conflict out of cowardice, cowardice makes you weaker. Grasp the nettle. As Sabine, an experienced manager and participant in one of our international leadership programmes once put it: "Sometimes, as a manager, you've got to have cojones. If your team is in conflict get a grip on your nerves and address the issues in your team. It gives you bigger cojones next time!"

It would be too easy to say: wimps shouldn't be leading project teams. Conflict management should be one of the team leader's core competencies. That's saying it to the point, but it's not true. There are clear differences between conventional and real project leaders. Which would you prefer to be?

Be a real team leader!

Conventional project leaders are very well aware that something is not quite right in the team. Often, they try to improve the mood without the help of the team. That is a mistake:

> Trying to lift the mood without engaging the team makes you look like an overly ambitious team doctor. Or worse still, like a court jester.

Successful team leaders don't try to lighten the mood single-handedly with comments like: "Ok, now don't despair! We'll manage. You'll see!" That doesn't work. You wouldn't buy that either, would you? Real team leaders know:

> The mood in the team is a task for the team.

One member of the team is rather annoyed? A real team leader doesn't try to talk him out of it. Instead he involves the entire team by asking what the problem is and how the issue can be resolved (if it's a more serious issue, then a 1:1 meeting is called for).

Less successful team leaders tend to complain more frequently about being 'torpedoed' by troublemakers in the team: "How do I get these guys back on track?" The question can't be answered because it's the wrong question. Successful team leaders ask an entirely different question: "How can I help the people in the team during the forming phase to find their position and role in the team?" Ask the question in this way and the answers will usually come by themselves.

Susanne, for instance, has a 'problem' with Chris because Chris always knows everything better. He seems to relish being a know-all. Consequently, Susanne doesn't label him as disruptive and doesn't fight him as that would just lead to escalation. Instead, she talks to him and asks if he'd like to be in charge of all issues concerning the technical implementation in the project in addition to his three work packages. He is quick to accept. From then on, he refrains from criticising project issues that are none of his business and where he really *doesn't* know it all. That's the way to form teams if you are good. How do you know you are good?

Hall of fame

From what we've discussed above, a number of key competencies become evident from the portfolio of a successful virtual leader:

- A 'normal' project leader focuses on his team. A (virtual) team leader focuses on his project and his team.
- A project leader plans his work packages. A team leader also plans the team's forming process.
- A project leader sees forming as a phase in the team's development. A team leader sees it as a key productivity factor.
- A project leader has a feeling for quality, scheduling, technology, capacity and finance. A team leader takes it a step further and keeps an eye on the team's mood.
- A project leader leads a project. A team leader, furthermore, is able to talk like a normal human being if the mood in the team needs him/her to.
- A project leader invests in technology and processes. A team leader invests in the team's forming too.
- A project leader complains about his team's performance, and hopes his team will eventually turn into a dream team.

- A team leader knows how to form the team him/herself as far as possible.

Conditio sine qua non

As soon as the buzzword 'forming' pops up, many top decision-makers become sceptical. An intelligent, successful project leader will ignore such scepticism. He knows:

> Where excellent forming is concerned, forming is the conditio sine qua non.

These are the conditions without which there can be no success. Achieving excellence means forming the team. It's your call and you'll rise to the occasion. Remember, it's not that difficult. In fact, it's easy but not simple. It's hard to achieve, not because of the complexity, but because it's unusual. Smart people practise forming with friends, relatives, family, colleagues or in their leadership roles. It always helps to gauge mood in such social constructs and to improve it either by addressing the issues, involving everyone in developing solutions or enabling interpersonal interactions.

In brief: Forming the team

- The better the forming, the more successful the project.
- Dream teams don't fall from heaven. They are formed.
- The best setting for this is the kick-off event.
- You don't have a budget? Then do your forming virtually.
- Use a pin-board, chat room, weekly team meeting, and agree on guidelines for communication and regular reflection.

- The most important elements of forming are: encouraging personal interaction; creating an infrastructure where interaction can take place (chat room, bulletin board …); mutual reflection; and influencing the emotional mood within the team.
- The essence of forming is: building trust by focusing on commonalities. Commonalities create team spirit. Discover and share the common ground!
- Ongoing forming: caring for the mood and trust level within the team!
- You're unsure about how to gauge the mood in the team? Don't worry. No great team leader was born with that ability. You learn that through experience and practice.
- The team is responsible for the team's mood and not you? Teams pull themselves together on their own? Mature and responsible adults should be able to get along with each other without outside help? Those are excuses, not team strategies.
- If you lack the communication competence to form the team professionally, there's a simple solution: learning by doing. Start by listening and asking questions.
- Don't resort to being Dr. Moodmaker or a court jester. Creating the right mood in the team is a task for the whole team.
- Enjoy yourself. It's easier than you think. Forming a team is twice the fun because you are creating both fun and success at the same time!

6. Influencing: The secret power

||||||||||||||||||||||||||||||||||||||||||||||||||||||||||

The power of the project leader

Managers have power (position power). That's why team members do as they are told. Usually project leaders don't have disciplinary powers and that's why...

- "... my team members just ignore me!"
- "... they only do what's absolutely necessary."
- "... they just do their own thing."
- "... I can't get on their cases if they don't deliver their work packages on time!"
- "... team members forego any kind of structure during video conferencing, turning the sessions into a free-for-all with a few talking shop, and the rest fiddling with their smartphones."
- "... people constantly take turns to arrive late for meetings."
- "... they listen politely but then turn around and do exactly what they think is right or they just do nothing. A project can't work like that. How could it?"

Good question. The project manager is the eunuch of the capitalist market economy. He would like to do many things but he doesn't have the required instruments. Conventional project management is difficult enough without formal power. A virtual leader has an even more difficult lot due to the distance and isolation of the team members! Which leadership instrument is there to fall back on in the absence of power and disciplinary authority? Many leaders really don't know. Even though leadership on the relationship level has such a catchy name:

Leading without power: influencing

Literally it means to assert influence. May I open your eyes? Anyone can do it. You can. You do already. Regardless of how powerful or powerless you may seem. Even the person who seems most unlikely to yield influence can have an influence on those around him/her. A typical example is an executive secretary. Officially they have no say in matters. In actual fact, however, smart secretaries are the silent power in departments, companies, unions, authorities and ministries. They influence their bosses, and consequently the whole team or organisation, more than their bosses can ever realise, although secretaries have no official disciplinary authority. They don't need it either; they know what to say and how to say it for their bosses to stay on track. The science of communication leverage is called influencing.

Leverage!

The good news is: influencing is nothing new, nor do you have to learn how to do it. You've already been doing it for some time. We all occasionally praise and show our appreciation in order to win people over. Everyone uses these and other influencing tools regularly, usually quite unconsciously. And therein lies the crux of the matter:

Unconscious influencing works. Conscious influencing works
even better.

When we influence others unconsciously, we generally use the three
preferred tools we are most used to using. Sometimes they work and
sometimes they don't. That's why there is a variety to choose from. Let's
take a look at the top ten influencing tools!

Develop your influencing toolbox so that you have more to
choose from in any given situation. You can ask yourself:
which tools will work best here? If it didn't work: what else
do I have in my toolbox?

Remember:

A quiver containing ten arrows is better than one with only
three.

Influencing is not comparable to a light switch that you turn on and off.
It's more like the organ in St. Paul's Cathedral: the more chords you hit
in succession, the easier it is to play music. Therefore:

Amateurs are disappointed if their counterpart doesn't
immediately react to an influencing tool. Professionals know
that it takes a combination of two, three or four tools to
achieve real impact.

Automatically and unconsciously pushing the same buttons time after time has another clear disadvantage: if you're always pushing the same old buttons, you're neither in tune with the situation nor with your counterpart. That's doomed to fail. Consider a basic maxim from the psychology of communication:

> If you keep doing what you've always been doing, then all you'll get is what you've always been getting.

This common approach won't get you anywhere. Going through life with the same three influencing tools lacks the flexibility for sustainable success:

> The closer you adapt your choice of influencing tools to the mood, the situation, the person or people you are dealing with, the higher the level of influence you will reach.

The more influencing tools in your toolbox the better. Let's take a look at the top ten, extensively researched tools.

1. Refer to a higher authority!

The appeal to authority works best with a counterpart who thinks hierarchically and is afraid of rocking the boat: "The boss said we should ..."; "We both know how the executive board feels about that ..."; "We both know what the boss would say ..."; "The steering committee will be furious if we do that!"; "You know how much the customer loves tech. He's sure to prefer the state-of-the-art version."; "I don't think our client will go for that ...".

Referring to authority is very powerful as most people are reluctant to cross swords with those in power positions

Of course, both external and internal experts are considered authorities: "McKinsey says …"; "In a study conducted by Roland Berger Strategic Partners …"; "The guys from Assist International HR recommend …" You don't like pushing others by referring to authorities? Then forget about this tool. Influencing is about:

> **Choosing the three to five tools that suit you, your counterpart and the situation.**

2. Join forces!

We're all familiar with so-called allying from advertising. Take for example the famous slogan 'Cats would buy Whiskas'. Why has it been so successful for all these years? Because it implies: so it's not just my cat but cats worldwide. That has a strong impact. More helps more. That's why, for instance, one project manager avoided saying: "I need the new PM software for this project!" and said instead: "The project team, the IT people, F&E and Production would prefer to do their planning with the new software." The effect is much stronger.

Is the boss likely to sense a mutiny behind allying because he's a paranoid choleric? "What are you guys plotting behind my back?" Then allying is obviously not right for your boss. So don't use it. Choose your tools wisely. Not every tool is suited to every situation. Choosing the right tool is at the very heart of influencing.

3. Emphasise the relationship!

Socialising. "How long have we known each other now?" "This is the third project we've been on together, right?" "It's great to be on a project with you again. What have you been up to in the meantime?" "I'm sure we can make this work. We're all in the same boat after all!"

Build on your relationship: draw upon past experiences, the stories you shared and your mutual ties. At the start of the critical meeting with the client, the project leader says, "On the way to today's meeting I was thinking: the last few months have been pretty tough for all of us, haven't they?" Isn't this manoeuvre just a bit too obvious?

Yes, it is. It's like presenting your host with a gift. We all know that the present is intended as a gesture of good will. So we accept graciously. That's what's so ingenious about influencing: the tools are so simple and yet so ingenious. It's just being able (and willing) to use them.

4. Give reasons!

Hunger in developing countries is increasing because speculators are driving the wheat prices up. Unfortunately, this isn't the whole truth. Droughts and crop failures over the last years have had a much greater influence on the prices. But most people believe it's the speculators' fault. Why? Because of the 'because'.

"There are three good reasons …", "That's the best solution because …" Regardless of whatever half-baked reasoning follows, it's going to have an effect because it was introduced as a reason in the beginning. That s our Gestalt perception. We hear the reasoning but not the content. And if you deliver three reasons in one breath, your influence triples. Plus, combining what is referred to as logical reasoning with other tools will increase your influence even more. For example: "That's the quickest solution and saves time. By the way, that's what the steering committee believes too. You know how keen they are to speed things up!"

A particularly effective and intellectually sophisticated form of reasoning is to refer to eternally valid and generally accepted values such as justice, fairness, social harmony, progress, prosperity, growth, security, health, humanity, effectiveness and harmony ... can you think of any more? Include this line of reasoning in your arguments. For example: "It's clearly unfair that the controllers are always correcting our forecast calculation and the marketing department is always allowed to stick to the same budget!" As a result, the marketing people are more likely to get moving in the right direction than if one were to badger them for the umpteenth time: "Could you please finally deliver your updated budget!"

5. Ask 'yes' questions!

Saying 'no' inevitably weakens your position of power. After five consecutive no's at the latest, you'll lose your audience. So make sure that you get as many yes's as possible. Telemarketers sometimes get it wrong: "Do you have a minute?" No, of course not; what a stupid question! "Would you say that paying by credit card simplifies paying bills? "Nine out of ten people questioned are likely to answer with 'yes'. Otherwise they wouldn't have credit cards.

Ask questions that are likely to elicit agreement or cooperation: "Do you agree that …?" Of course, it's better to steer clear of far-fetched questions and stick to those that relate to the subject or something that matters to the person: "Arsenal got off to a cracking start to the season, didn't they?" Once you agree to harmless questions, you are more likely to go along with the more controversial ones. That makes sense. Unfortunately, all too often it's not put into practice. Why? Because most people focus on the points of contention straight away. "Why are you against bringing in an external supplier to construct the gear units?" Why do smart people make such stupid mistakes? Because they think 'logically', are goal-oriented and communicate effectively. Or at least, that's what they believe.

A further development of the 'yes' question is the intention question. A lot of managers try desperately to 'convince' and 'motivate' with persuasive argumentation: "Just do it like I told you. That's the best way forward." That hardly convinces anybody. It persuades at best. Much stronger than attempts at persuading are intention questions. For example: "Which better approach do you know? And why, from your point of view, is that better?" Asking a question in this way lets the receiver 'convince' him/herself, or opens the way for productive and mutually beneficial problem-solving.

6. Appreciate!

The entire transfer problem of influencing becomes apparent where showing appreciation, or 'valuing' is concerned. We have known since our earliest school days that we should appreciate and respect each other. But we don't do it. That's one reason why appreciation is so effective. It's a rare commodity in today's world. People spend all day at work, working their fingers to the bone in order to support their families and what do they get for it? Not only is there little appreciation, but instead they are lambasted or ignored. How often during an average working day do you get the feeling that you are an asset to the company? That's why appreciation works. The person being appreciated considers it a fair trade: "I do something and get something in return, namely appreciation." Furthermore, it just feels good to be appreciated. Being on the receiving end of appreciation just feels really good.

Alan, for example, simply forgets that when he calls Björn in Kiel and jumps right in: "You have cover for me! Our investor wants us to present the new hydraulic system on site, and I can't get away from the R&D centre in time!" Whereupon Björn responds rather dryly: "I don't have to do anything. The presentation is in three days' time! Do you think I have nothing to do here? I have my own long-term scheduling that I can't simply rearrange because you guys in London are having another one of your scheduling fiascos!" Total rejection. Fortunately, Alan recalls the crash course he took in influencing together with other project leaders last summer upon the recommendation of a clever HR developer in his company.

That's why Alan is quick to follow up his faux pas with some valuing. He adds something which should always be included when one asks a favour from someone: appreciation and acknowledgement. He adds: "I'm sorry … you're right. You don't *have* to do anything. I know you've got a lot on your plate yourself at the moment. But if you help me now, you'll save my life. The executive board keeps telling me how important this investor is to our company (appeal to authority). You'd really be saving my bacon!" Ok, that's all a bit exaggerated, but as far as appreciation goes, you can and should exaggerate a little. It used to be called sweet talking, and it works. Björn grumbles around for a couple of minutes, but then acquiesces. Influencing accomplished.

Show your counterpart you appreciate them. Exaggerate the value of what they do for you moderately, or strongly. That sounds simple enough. However, we tend not to practise this in our daily lives. That's why most of us are not very good at it. So what can you do? Start by practising valuing in innocuous situations. Why don't most intelligent and educated people do that? Because in the greater part of the Western world, showing appreciation is perceived as a weakness. Being too nice comes across as soft. That's the worry people have. The opposite is true, but then there are a lot of worried people in management.

7. Inspire!

"We are a really fabulous team. We really Get Sh*t Done! We are changing our customer's world. Management sees us as an invaluable asset, and the executive committee has us on their radar. So let me ask you: would you like to join our project team?"

Who wouldn't after such an inspiring pitch? Inspiring is another influencing tool that most of us see the point of immediately. But many of us are unable to put it into practice. In the Western daily work and family routine, the belief holds: anyone who goes around enthusiastically motivating others is not all there. Those who don't complain around the clock about one thing or another are seen as annoyingly complacent. It keeps us from showing too much enthusiasm and inspiring others. That and too little practice. Actually that's a good thing. Just imagine how much faster and easier you could succeed if, with very little practice, you were able to inspire others much easier and faster than the poker-faced pessimists around you! Take Sandra for example.

After four hours of intense discussion she says: "Ok, I think we can wrap up the discussion at this point. We've found our solution." By that time, most of those at the table seem to have switched off and stopped listening. So she switches to inspiring and adds: "That's the best solution I can imagine. It's taken four hours of difficult discussion to reach it. The customer will love it. It's exactly what he was asking for. He'll be forever grateful once he sees this." The discussion stops abruptly. All eyes are upon her as if asking: do you mean that? It's that good?

How do you inspire? That's the question I get asked most by people who have long since had any inspiration driven out of them in their routine workday. So that's the answer: see things from the others' perspective. Don't ask yourself: how can I inspire him/her? Ask instead: what is he/she enthusiastic about? What's important to him/her? What makes his/

her heart beat faster? Practise that with family members and don't be surprised if you discover entirely new sides.

8. Be a role model!

If the project leader doesn't deliver on time, his team members aren't likely to do so either. Why? Because the project leader sets an example. Whether he likes it or not. If that is the case, he/she can deliberately apply so-called role modelling. Walk your talk and demonstrate the behaviour you would like to see in others!

Of course that makes sense. It contradicts the human inclination to demand from others what one can't or is unwilling to deliver oneself. A fitting saying here is: do as I say, don't do as I do! In other words, act in accordance with my words and not my actions. Of course, the right words are important if I want the work to be delivered on time, and I have to tell my people constantly. Often that's not enough. What works is if they see me arriving or delivering on time. If the project leader insists on everyone beginning at telcos on time, and then dials in late on every other telco, it's pretty clear what that will lead to.

9. You scratch my back!

Manus manum lavat. Or, one hand washes the other. You scratch my back and I'll scratch yours. Since that's a given, you apply it and call it exchanging. That goes back to the Romans: *do ut des*! Give, so that you receive. Or, in real time: "Do me a favour and I'll owe you one!" In corporations, these are the unofficial channels, also called networking. Everything the official organisation structure doesn't achieve due to arthritic decision-making can be achieved by a well-oiled network of mutually indebted colleagues. That works extremely well in practice.

Recently, I happened to overhear a conversation between a project leader and a member of the team: "I'm quite aware that I'm in no position to give orders. I'm not your boss. But if you resolve this issue for me, I'll make sure that the steering committee finds out exactly who got us out of this fix." You're right. It sounds like a double whammy of exchanging and valuing (see 6)!

10. Say what you want to happen!

Most people don't express their wishes clearly. They beat about the bush when they want something or hint vaguely, hoping that their counterpart will grasp the gist of the request on their own. That is doomed to failure.

In her last telco, for example, Zoe said: "That needs to be taken care of." Will it be? Forget it. Two weeks after the telco nothing has changed. Zoe's mentor gives her a subtle hint: "You've got to tell the people very politely and very clearly what you expect them to do!" In one word: declaring. So in the next telco she says: "I'd like for our construction people to complete that by tomorrow please." The three construction guys on the team reply: "That's impossible! We can manage it by the day after tomorrow at best!" Zoe thinks to herself: Job Done.

Why do people find it so difficult to say what they want to happen? This is often because they confuse three terms: polite, direct and clear. "That won't work" is a direct statement. It just isn't clear what you mean by it. Why won't that work? And what indeed would work? Some cultures – Germans, Scandinavians and North Americans for example – are known for their directness and often think they've made themselves absolutely clear. That's not necessarily the case. If we need something, the best way to get what we want is to be clear *and* polite – not direct.

Beware of negative influencers!

All the influencing tools we've briefly outlined are both simple and ingenious, especially compared to those tools we often habitually, spontaneously and unconsciously apply to get what we want. Take emotional blackmail for example: "Please do me the favour, or the customer will bite my head off!" You may well do him the favour, but both of you are likely to feel uncomfortable about it, because you sense you have just been emotionally blackmailed. That leaves a bitter aftertaste and has a negative effect on the relationship. This is a particularly bad idea in virtual teams, where maintaining relationships is difficult enough due to distance and isolation.

The same is true for applying pressure and threatening with consequences: "If it isn't ready by the beginning of next week the customer is going to give us hell!" Threats like that are common, however they wear off over time, destroy team morale and are entirely unnecessary, particularly since you've just been introduced to a whole bunch of constructive alternatives which influence your team colleagues and boost team spirit at the same time. Pressure is not a leveraging tool, even if many managers seem to think it is. Pressure creates counter-pressure. Typically, managers in a position of power tend to exert pressure. Their position power base blinds them to the side effects caused by pressure: power kills the motivation to learn. That's one reason why despots are toppled sooner or later: they aren't able to learn new things fast enough.

Undoubtedly, the most popular of these unreflected 'killers' are the pseudo-influencers: nagging, griping, acting like a prima donna and moaning. Just take a look at the amount of moaning in Western Europe! "We'll never make it! The deadline is much too tight, and we haven't got enough budget!" That may all be true, but how is whining and complaining about it going to change things? Don't be fooled!

Don't be a whiner! Be an influencer!

The choice of weapons

You've just been introduced to the top 10 influencing tools. When do you choose which tool? That depends on three questions:

1) Does this tool suit your style?
2) Does it fit the subject or the situation?
3) Is it right for your counterpart?

What suits you? If you are a relatively shy or reserved person, you might not want to start with inspiring (see no. 7) straight way, unless of course you're inspired to do so and want to try it out. Well, then it might suit you after all. What else suits your style? Have a think about which three tools are your current unconscious favourites and ask yourself which other tools would complement them best. You can also ask yourself which ones you'd like to try out. The main thing is that you know how to use them, and they feel right to you.

In addition, the tool should suit the subject matter and the situation. Socialising (no. 3), for instance, works especially well within the team context: "How long have the two of us been with this organisation? I'd say we know how things are done around here ..."

Of course, each tool has to be appropriate for your counterpart. This prerequisite is the underlying principle of every communication, which politicians, supervisors with official authority, journalists, significant others, mothers-in-law and despots seem to continually enjoy violating: you need to know your counterpart well enough to understand what suits them best and what doesn't. This is a pretty straightforward basis for successful influencing, which a surprising number of people seem to be blissfully unaware of. For example, trying to influence a university professor with the research results of a rival faculty (see no. 1, Appeal to authority), is not going to bring the desired results: no professor will tolerate authorities beside him/herself. Role modelling (see no. 8) also won't work in this case: he/she simply won't accept you as a role model. You may well have more luck by placing the boot on the other foot and turning him into a role model. For example: "If you, as a renowned expert in the field, were in favour of behavioural economics, then I'm sure our executive board will find it much easier to agree!"

Which tool works best when? You're the one who knows that best. Be your own personal guru! Keep track: note which tool worked well with whom in what situation and with whom it didn't work. That's the best way to document your personal hit list. Moreover, you realise automatically which tools you are subconsciously drawn to. Which ones do you still 'forget' about too often? Which ones should you use more often?

In brief: Influence!

- You have no formal power in the project. You don't need that kind of power.
- There is something much better! Influencing.
- Play the ten influencing tools like a piano virtuoso.

  1. Refer to a higher authority!
  2. Join forces with others!
  3. Emphasise the relationship!
  4. Give logical reasons!
  5. Ask questions that elicit agreement or cooperation!
  6. Appreciate!
  7. Inspire!
  8. Be a role model!
  9. Offer favours in exchange!
  10. State what you want or need clearly and politely!

"I didn't realise how important trust is to the team's
productivity until it was too late."

Adele S., team leader

7. The team accelerator: Trust

|||||||||||||||||||||||||||||||||||||||||||||||||||||

The misery of mistrust

What would it take to make your team faster? Perform better? More
efficient? Would it take a bigger budget? Better experts? No, that's not it.
Most people believe that's what it takes but only a cherished few work
out what the team accelerator really is. Not even Sarah.

While we're talking, Sarah's mailbox buzzes: mail from Pablo in Ma-
drid. She sees who the mail is from, turns to her office colleague and,
with raised eyebrows, says: "Oh no, not that Spanish guy again. What
does he want this time?" She hasn't even read the first line of the mail
but Sarah's spontaneous team reaction kicks in: mistrust – and she's
not the only one. In at least three quarters of her team there is a high
level of mistrust. We are all familiar with this kind of pronounced
caution towards our colleagues. We all encounter this occasionally with our teammates. Isn't that normal? The question in itself is
worrying enough.

> Many people sense the latent mistrust in teams (families, parties, clubs, nations), but they consider it 'normal' (as if a nosebleed were normal). They don't see it as a potential risk or the cause of friction within the team or as a handbrake on project team effectiveness.

Can't they see it or don't they want to see it? It's usually because people are conditioned to be unable to see it. Managers are conditioned to focus on numbers, data and facts all through their careers. It's only the Bottom Dollar that counts. That's where their focus is. Which on the one hand is a good thing. On the other hand, the focus on numbers, data and facts means that everything else slips off the radar. Many leaders are de facto blind to the mistrust within their teams. They are either unaware of it or they don't take it seriously. Either way, they're heading for trouble.

In my work, I frequently encounter team leaders who make any number of unbelievable professional and project management gaffes, but their teams deliver excellent results because the team's culture of trust is able to iron things out. Team members think and say: "Ah, what the heck ... he's our team leader. These things happen; we'll work it out for him. It's really about give and take, isn't it?" On the other hand, I encounter team managers who are acknowledged experts and run a tight ship where their projects are concerned. Nevertheless, they always seem to lag behind schedule because team members often work against each other instead of with each other. Because they don't trust each other.

> Trust is the foundation of team success.

That may have caused you to roll your eyes. I often hear comments such as: "Trust is such an abstract concept! What does it really mean?" That's a good question. Try asking yourself that question. No, in fact, let me ask you.

Whom do you trust?

Trust: is it that important? Of course, if you trust one another, the going is smoother. But if you don't, what do you really lose? We all have our instructions and guidelines to follow after all, so trust is not that much of an issue. Most people seem to think that. Until they ask themselves this:

> Do you trust your partner? Your parents? Your doctor? Your coach? What is the impact if you don't? Which people in your life do you really trust? Does that trust have a meaning for you? How small or how great is that significance? What impact does this trust have on your interactions, communication and transactions with the people you're dealing with? What would happen if this trust suddenly turned to mistrust? Do you treat people you trust differently from those you mistrust?

Did that make you think? Going deeper, here's another question:

> Do you like working with people you don't trust?

In 9 out of 10 cases the answer is: "No, I don't!" For 4 in 10 cases, awareness of the underlying meaning of trust is acute enough that the answer is: "I not only don't like working with people I don't trust, but work is considerably less effective." That's a steadfast law of virtual leadership:

Teams with a culture of mistrust deliver sub-standard results.

It's logical. Mistrust leads to friction, it slows the teamwork down and kills efficiency.

Mistrust is a soft factor with extremely tough consequences.

Soft factor, hard facts

If you aren't aware of this, you don't see the consequences of mistrust. Fortunately, Brigitte is aware.

She recounts: "We reach our work package interfaces three times as fast as other teams." How do you do it? Brigitte explains: "Before the work packages are delivered there are issues that need to be clarified. If there is a climate of mistrust, the person receiving the work packages puts the brakes on, leaving the packages to wait, on the principle that 'I won't touch this until everything has been clarified!'" Whereupon the team plunges into endless discussions along the lines of: "That's not what we agreed to! I'm not delivering this package until it has been revised!"

Which symptoms of mistrust do you have in your team? None? Are you sure? They are always lurking somewhere. The question is: are you attuned to them? And are the symptoms mild, borderline, toxic or even lethal?

Brigitte's team, for instance, shows only a few symptoms of mistrust. Delivering work packages is usually accompanied by the following dialogue:

"Alex, today's the deadline for delivery, but my work package isn't really ready. We've had to work around the specifications because things just weren't going according to plan. I'm really sorry. What do you suggest we do now?" – "Don't worry Lisa. We'll just get started and you explain the changes to me as we go along." Delivery of the work packages runs its course without any kind of friction. While other teams are still discussing how to proceed, Brigitte's team is already hard at work. The reason why her team can move forward so quickly is that members are supportive of one another. And that only works if there is a solid foundation of trust. How come Alex and Lisa trust each other? Or, should we ask how did Brigitte manage to create a trusting bond between Alex and Lisa? How does a team leader create that very necessary, efficiency boosting factor of trust within the team?

Creating trust

"If trust is so important, then why don't team members just trust each other?" This is a favourite question that steering committees like to ask me. What a question! Married couples don't automatically start trusting each other just because the priest says: "You may now kiss the bride!" So why not? The answer is quite obvious:

> Trust is not something you can expect or assume or order.
> It has to be developed and maintained.

How? Or indeed, where? You already know the answer:

> The kick-off is the first and most significant trust-building measure.

Ok, we all know that now: the kick-off is the answer to (almost) all questions related to virtual leadership. But why? Put simply, how come team members go into a kick-off with mistrust and leave with established trust among the team members? What happens during the kick-off?

Well, just that: trust-building. How is it done? That's a really good question. Do you know the answer? Think about it. Management gurus have been preaching since Moses came down from the mountain how important trust is. So we should know how to generate this all-important trust. What's your bet?

Don't blame yourself. Not many people have the answer. The answer is one word: commonalities.

> Bonding creates trust. The more commonalities people find, the stronger the trusting bond.

Does that sound too easy, too trivial? Believe me, I hear these objections a lot. That's the reason why there is so much mistrust in the business world. Modern man has long since forgotten what was taken for granted by our Neanderthal ancestors: only trust those with whom you share commonalities!

This is exactly the reason why well-functioning kick-offs include icebreaking introductory sessions, a ritual that many find silly. Of course, it is totally irrelevant for the project's technical, scheduling and financial issues if Zoe goes horse riding in her free time, or Florence loves line dancing. But it *does* make a difference where mutual trust is concerned. These bits of 'irrelevant' information are extremely relevant as both realise during the round of introductions: "Hey! He/she likes sports just as much as I do!" That's where trust starts. Sure, that's really trivial! But then that's the way we humans tick. I didn't invent it.

It's the tragedy of the 21st century business world that current business teachings have all but relegated these fateful acts of triviality to the back burner! Don't make the same mistake. Design introductory sessions in your kick-off (or your first meeting) with the primary focus on the discovery of what the team members have in common. The lead should be: "Tell me about yourself, so I can find out where you and I are alike." The more commonalities, the stronger the trust bond will be, and the more likely it is that your teammate will become your friend and trusted partner. Many team leaders are aware of this, and what do they do?

Right, they go bowling in the evening. That's a well-meant gesture, but it doesn't work. When you go bowling that's what you do: you bowl. Discovering commonalities becomes a side attraction, beyond bowling, of course. Finding out what you have in common is top priority for the success of the team. It's not just a nice-to-have social interlude that can be fitted in nicely between dinner and the late news. And it was at one such introductory kick-off that Lisa and Alex first got to know each other and discovered a handful of commonalities. That's how they began trusting each other. That's why their collaboration is twice as effective and efficient as the work done by team members in other teams.

The trust base Lisa and Alex share is definitely an asset. Trust, however, is not that one-dimensional. It's also multi-layered. In virtual high-performing teams, team members:

- share a common goal,
- trust their team leader,
- and (to an extent) also their customer,
- trust the flow of information in the team,
- trust each other.

How can you achieve this multi-dimensional trust? Without a kick-off? There's a double strategy to get there: keep trying to persuade the kick-off sceptics, and at the same time, work on building trust without the help of a kick-off. How? Like I say, trust is created through commonalities and can, if needs must, be nurtured without the help of a kick-off in regular meetings and telcos. No one can forbid you from engaging in an introductory session in your first meeting … and no one can forbid you from feeding the cat.

"Feed the cat!"

Men are often accused of no longer making an effort to please their wives once the marriage papers have been signed and the 'goal' has been 'successfully' reached. Men are not alone in thinking competitively. "Goal attained and success celebrated. Job done. Bring on the next challenge!" That works really well with many challenges, but definitely not with relationships, marriages, families, children, pets, and trust. And not just that. It's counterproductive.

> Trust is like physical fitness, endurance, strength, self-confidence: it needs constant maintenance.

There are just things you have to do every day. Brush your teeth, wash the dishes, feed the cat and nurture trust. It's not complicated and it doesn't take much effort:

> Provide your team members with different and regular opportunities to nurture their commonalities informally. It has a stabilising effect and strengthens the bond of trust.

Encourage your team members to talk about their commonalities. Take the opposite route to your line managers: "What? You're exchanging recipes? Are you out of your mind? That's not what I pay you for!" One team leader, on the other hand, who was aware of the importance of trusting his team, reacted quite differently to the situation: "What did you say our Indian colleague mailed you? His recipe for original chicken tikka masala? Please forward it to me! I really like spicy food. And while you're at it, please ask him for a recipe for a typical Indian dessert!" Abracadabra, like magic, the sense of trust in the team leader has increased. "Hey, the guy likes Indian food, like we do. He's like us!" That's how it works in high-performance team.

This is hardly surprising to those who are familiar with the close friendship and trust among members of a winning sports team. Their bond is necessarily one of friendship and trust. Colleagues work together, whether they like it or not. Friends trust and cover for one another; they support each other and avoid the typical mistrust games played by many poorly performing teams: "What does he want this time? I wonder what she meant by that? What is he up to?" At the risk of repeating myself:

Foster trust in the team by offering enough opportunities for discovering and nurturing commonalities.

These days, many organisations have Intranet and Internet platforms for their teams, where teams can find all the data, plans, charts, work methods, forms, and overviews pertaining to their projects. Team-oriented corporations set up chat rooms for members to share ideas and personal interests. That's trust-building.

Don't leave trust-building to the Internet or the team members alone. As the team leader you have so much influence on the trust-building dynamic in the team. Build on this influence.

The chief trust builder

Trust among team members is all the stronger:

- the more you appreciate the contributions made by your teammates. Avoid, for example: "But we've already tried that!" Instead try: "Good idea, sounds familiar. Can you tell us more?"
- In other words, the more you work on mastering your Pacing & Leading skills. Always appreciate what your counterpart has said before giving your own opinion. The most relationship-friendly way to do this is in the form of a question.
- the more consistent you are in acknowledging good work. Instead of: "Finished your work package yet? Good." Try instead: "Ah, your work package is two days late? Ok, well, I really liked the way you solved that technical issue. Great job." You can actually watch the recipient growing a few inches taller. Nothing inspires trust more than "he/she appreciates what I've achieved!"
- the more constructively you address problems, mistakes and setbacks. So instead of saying: "It's still not working? Get a move on!" Try instead: "Oh, so that didn't work out either? What are you going to try next? Good to see you are so committed on this."
- the more you withhold overused generalisations about trust. Instead of: "Go ahead, I trust you!" refer to something more specific in terms of particular plans/achievements: "I don't have a ready-made solution for that either. How do you want to go about it? Aha, good idea. Give it a try!"
- the more open and honest you are in your communication. Instead of: "I have no idea what the steering committee intends to do with it!" say: "They may well place our project results in mothballs. But it's much better to have a great result gathering dust than a lousy one."
- the more team members can count on your availability ("Don't trust anyone who's never there!").

- the more opportunities you have to nurture commonalities, and the more you get involved and show your team members: "We have something in common in that respect! I think and feel the same as you on that issue!"

Open and honest communication in project management? Some of you will have laughed out loud when you read that. Your mirth is justified. Trust is such a valuable commodity, that the requirements for building trust are significant. Honesty (6), the ability and willingness to give positive feedback (3), a constructive approach to addressing mistakes (4), highly disciplined scheduling (7). Hand on heart: Do you know many line managers who fulfil these criteria? Neither do I. Which means we can draw the following interesting conclusions:

- Line managers lead with power and discipline – excellent team leaders lead by trust.
- Because of this trust factor, good team leaders are the better managers.
- Virtual team leaders have to fulfil higher requirements than line managers and normal team leaders. That's what makes them special!
- Put simply: a virtual leader is the better leader.
- It would be great if this awareness were to reach the personnel and management development departments! A manager has been sufficiently developed when he has become adept at leading virtually.
- If you can lead a virtual team you can lead anything.
- Virtual leadership is the elite training centre for managers.
- Virtual leadership is the black belt of leadership judo.

If you implement these 7 tips, you will automatically become the better leader, and, for that matter, more successful, well-liked, and trustworthy. That sounds good doesn't it? It's certainly worth the effort. One of these tips, however, deserves further attention. It's called availability:

Don't trust anyone who is never there!

Some people may believe that to be considered truly trustworthy, one has to be as virtuous as Gandhi, as genuine as the Dalai Lama, and as honest as Abraham "Honest Abe" Lincoln. Sure, honesty counts. But you don't have to be a Nobel Peace Prize winner to earn your team's trust:

> Contextual factors are stronger than behavioural components.

This is best exemplified by taking a look at diets. Studies by nutritionists show that those who succeed are not necessarily those with the strongest willpower (behaviour!), but those with the smaller plates (context). Sticking to a diet does not require a will of iron, as that is likely to start to crumble after the first four weeks. Evidence suggests that using smaller plates will automatically lead to eating smaller portions and thus less food intake. This requires a fraction of the willpower. Just go out and buy a new set of plates! Ergo:

> You're looking to build trust in your team? Create the context!

Assume you dent the bumper of your car. Then your kid throws a stone through the glass roof of your neighbour's greenhouse. In both cases, and after several attempts, you are unable to reach your insurance agent. How much do you trust this insurance company? Quite simply – you don't: "They're not reliable!" Which isn't true: They're just not available. However, we often equate availability with trustworthiness and reliability (generally referred to as Fundamental Attribution Error). In other words:

Unclear or unregulated availability kills trust, especially in virtual teams, where you can't just go down the hall and pop into a team member's office to get information. So define consistent and transparent availability!

That's how to ensure trustful teamwork. Without fostering this contextual factor, trust within the team will eventually dissipate. "But my spouse/girlfriend/boyfriend will kill me if I am available to my team members around the clock!" is a lament I hear from many project leaders. Who says you have to be?

The feeling of having to be on call at all times is a major stress factor and burn-out driver for many employees in today's business world. Even though the problem could be solved really easily:

You don't have to be available all the time, just reliably available

An open-door policy is not the solution, nor are consultation hours from 7:00 a.m. to 6:00 p.m. In fact, it's counterproductive and ineffective. Monika, a very accomplished team leader, for example, has set a daily telephone time aside for her project team X from 10:00–11:00 a.m. only. If one hour isn't enough, she schedules a follow-up appointment. Everyone in the team knows that for this one hour, she is reliably and one-hundred percent available. That's enough – provided it applies to all team members. That's why you should reach an agreement with your team on:

- who is definitely available at what time on what day of the week?
- what are the emergency arrangements outside of these hours? E-Mail? Text message?

- In your team, agree that if you can't keep a defined availability time slot, you will inform all others ahead of time!

Experienced project leaders distribute a telephone list that includes the members' respective availability. This helps to set a dependable contextual frame and creates trust.

No favouritism!

What creates trust within the team? The best answers to this question can be found if you turn it around:

What is the fastest way to squander trust?

That's easy. Just give your 'teacher's pet' preferential treatment. Be careful. It can happen to any of us at any time unintentionally and without thinking about it. Most of the time, we're not even aware of it, but our team members are. Hannah, for example, says: "If we don't deliver the advertising material as quickly as expected, the project leader really gets on my case. The technicians, on the other hand, can do no wrong. They're the project leader's pets. That sucks." Ergo: the trust goes right down the drain. Hannah and her colleagues in Marketing trust neither the project manager nor the technicians.

> **Favouritism kills trust.**

Trust flourishes where there's fairness and justice. If you give some team members preferential treatment, those who feel disadvantaged withdraw their trust in you. Be sure to treat all members equally! That's not easy, because we all automatically like some people better than others, and that's exactly the point:

A leader merits the definition because he/she doesn't follow personal preference and chemistry and leads according to generally accepted, effective leadership principles instead.

One of the principles states just that: avoid preferential treatment. Since we do this unconsciously anyway, it takes conscious countermeasures:

You know exactly whom you like better and automatically prefer a little over others. There's no need to try and suppress this inclination entirely (nor can you, for that matter). Just counter it by making a conscious effort to address and engage those team members who aren't on the top of your likeability list.

Max, for instance, goes with his team colleagues to watch Newcastle United home games from time to time, because his office in Newcastle. That doesn't help, because the Liverpool faction of the team grumbles audibly:

"When he does manage to show up here on business, he doesn't as much as invite us out for a beer!" So you're getting upset over a pint of beer?

Yes, that's the way people are. You can ignore it. That's called management. Or you can choose not to ignore it. That's called leadership. It's your choice. Max made his decision, and sent the eight members of his Liverpool team an email: "After-work meeting at the Red Lion next Thursday at 6:00 p.m. The table is booked. Hope to see you all there. And leave your cars at home." Thirty seconds after the email arrived, the mood at the Liverpool office improved noticeably. Remember: teams consist of human beings, regardless of management practices that ask employees to leave their human selves at the door when they clock in. Human beings expect to be treated as such. In line-managed teams this can be ignored chronically and notoriously, but not in a project.

Especially not in a virtual project! Trust in your team and continue to build on that trust! This might sound a bit too touchy-feely, but it's really worth the effort. Trust is the glue that holds every virtual team together.

In brief: Create trust!

- Mistrust spreads like wildfire in virtual teams.
- Sharpen your senses for the mistrust level in your team. Which symptoms do you recognise?
- Don't fight the mistrust. Build and nurture trust instead. That's both more efficient and more effective.
- Your first opportunity for trust-building: the kick-off.
- The most important element of trust-building: personal interaction among team members as well as between the team members and the team leader.
- The key question to focus on is: what do we have in common?
- The more commonalities you find together, the stronger the trust factor will be in the team.
- Reserve consistently at least 10% of all mails, phone calls, telcos, messages and meetings to nurture common interests.
- Trust needs regular nurturing. Once lost it's too late.
- Team leaders have considerable influence on the trust in the team. the more you acknowledge your team members' every concern; the more you express appreciation for a job well done; the more the feedback concerning errors you give is constructive and relationship-oriented; the more you communicate openly and honestly; the more commonalities you share with team members;

and the more you are reliably available, the more the team will trust you.

- The more dependably each member's availability is clearly established, the stronger the trust factor within the team. Ergo, agree on terms of availability!
- Avoid all favouritism!
- Activate your inner critic each time you communicate with your team, and ask yourself the question: how will what I'm about to say impact the trust factor in the team? How could I reformulate it to strengthen the trust level?

> "There are two ways of meeting difficulties: You alter
> the difficulties or you alter yourself meeting them."
>
> Phyllis Bottome

8. The power of conflict

Most conflicts are avoidable

What slows teams down? It's strange how often team leaders complain about delays without asking why. Why? Because one involuntarily and erroneously assumes one knows the reason for the delay: "He's usually so reliable!" Oh, ok, and now he's suddenly 'unreliable'? That's a classic case of erroneous attribution:

> Don't blame delays on character weaknesses. Instead, look
> for the underlying conflict.

In fact, the 'unreliable' colleague hadn't succumbed to a sudden attack of unreliability. Half-way through the work package he had become involved in a quarrel with one of his colleagues, whose support he had been counting on. The conflict cost him valuable time and caused the consequent delay. The team leader, however, is unaware of this. All he sees is the delay and not the underlying conflict that caused it.

> You can't manage what you can't see: if your team isn't performing as expected – look for underlying conflicts!

There are not more conflicts in virtual teams than in conventional teams. They just get recognised later. That's why it seems as if there are actually more. Conflict kills team performance. But no one readily admits that, until the sh*t hits the fan. What do most people say at that point? Well, they say: "I don't believe it! How can we have lost so much time over this kerfuffle? It's so unnecessary!" Worse still: it's absolutely avoidable.

> Most conflicts are avoidable.

A virtual leader who is worth his salt doesn't spend time running around putting out fires. He's ahead of the game, because even in conflict situations he maintains the lead. He manages conflict *before* it erupts in full force. How does he do it? You know the answer by now:

> The better the team members get to know each other,
> the lower the conflict potential.

Have you noticed? Another strong argument in favour of a kick-off, and a good piece of advice for team leaders: the better the team knows you personally, the fewer issues and the fewer serious issues between team and team leader.

> Ensure that you and your team engage in personal interaction
> throughout the project regularly and from day one.

An effective element of this kind of interaction to prevent conflict is the so-called 'wall of fame'. This is a virtual bulletin board on the Internet where each team member posts a photo and introduces him- or herself personally (hobbies, likes, sports, food, literature, music ...). Sharing personal information of this kind fosters an unwillingness to attack: if I know someone shares my affinity for 80s music, for example, I'll be less likely to go for the person's throat than I might be with a perfect stranger. Commonalities bond (see chapter 5, People who are like each other like each other). The longer the project, the better people should know each other, and the more important regular interaction is. Getting to know people is a classic context factor (see chapter 7):

> It is easier to manage context than behaviour: "Don't argue! Please be reasonable!" Requests like that usually fall on deaf ears, because they're geared towards managing behaviour. However, if you create opportunities for your team members to get to know each other better (creating the context), there's no need to appeal to reason because serious conflict occurs less often.

There is another context factor with which you can manage conflict before it erupts: team goals.

Goals, goal criteria, responsibilities

Do you know why (see chapter 3) we have invested so much energy into formulating common team objectives? If team members just have goals dumped on them, they are unlikely to identify with them and more likely to argue. If, on the other hand, the team is involved in defining the objectives, the sense of ownership is increased and the motivation for conflict decreases.

> **Team members who 'own' the goals argue less.**

There is one more effect of common team objectives that inhibits conflict. Can you guess what that is? Here's a hint: what is one of the most common causes of team conflict? Right: "Hey, that wasn't what we agreed!" This objection is most often heard when a work package is designated and the recipient turns it down: "That wasn't what we agreed!" Ergo:

> **The more clearly you agree on (not dictate) goals, the more unlikely and the less severe the conflicts.**

Unfortunately, many team leaders are not particularly realistic when assessing the clarity of goals: "It's ok. Everyone knows what's expected of them." More often than not, that's not the case. How does that happen? What would you say?

> **Goals have only been clearly agreed upon when the acceptance criteria have been agreed upon too.**

Robert says to Claire: "I need your market analysis by September 25th, ok?" Would you let that count as a goal agreement? No! Why not? Because the acceptance criteria are missing. Consequently, Claire delivers an analysis on September 25th. Robert explodes: "That's not what I had in mind at all! It goes without saying that I need the data for Asia in addition to Central Europe!" So why didn't he say that to begin with? Because he's thinking in terms of goals ('market analysis'), but not in terms of acceptance criteria ('Europe and Asia').

State clearly: "This work package will be accepted if it meets the following acceptance criteria ...". Then agree on the criteria with the person responsible for the package.

This makes sense. Unfortunately, it's rarely practised. A frequent excuse is: "We're dealing with adults, after all. I feel like I'm micro-managing them. They know what's expected of them." That's illusion, not management. You can't lead a team like that. If you would like to sail through the project with a minimum of friction, you need clear and traceable criteria. And one more thing. Can you guess?

What is one of the most frequent causes of conflict in teams? That's right: the responsibilities. Something goes wrong, and fingers point in the direction of a colleague who responds: "Not my fault! That's not my responsibility!" Needless to say, the arguing begins about who could or should have been responsible. That's embarrassing and can be avoided:

Agree from the start on all the relevant responsibilities in as clear and detailed a way as possible. Be diplomatic and engage your team members in the process to avoid them feeling spoon-fed or pressured.

Goals, goal criteria and responsibilities – agree on these issues and half the conflict potential is defused once and for all. What about the other half?

The Cohn principle

I don't know why conflict management is considered by many to be 'complicated'. Basically, it's quite easy:

If team members talk to each other openly, there is no conflict, only differences of opinion.

Conflict doesn't occur out of the blue. Somebody is upset with someone for days or weeks before the actual conflict outburst. Why don't people talk to each other? It seems people prefer to sit on their hands, letting feelings of resentment seethe until they inevitably erupt in conflict. Ruth Cohn, the founder of theme-centred interaction, was so incensed by this inhibition against speaking up and the tendency to wallow in self-inflicted helplessness, that she 'devised' one of the best prophylactic measures. Quite simply it states:

Disruptions have priority!

Pin this core premise of conflict management on the virtual bulletin board! Address it at the very first team meeting (ideally at the kick-off event). Explain what it means. For example:

Don't try to smooth over disruptions! Always get them out in the open!

High-performance teams quite often include the following maxim in the agenda of their first meeting:

We agree to address possible differences of opinion as early as possible to prevent escalation and conflict.

That's easier said than done, of course. Especially since we've all been taught by parents and teachers to look away quickly and hope for divine providence to intervene if we sense the first sign of conflict. Or alternatively, to forget our manners and let loose with a verbal onslaught. That's why you should clarify the following points together with your team at the very first meeting:

- How can we address differences of opinion without stepping on someone's toes?
- What underlying toxic formulations should be avoided under all circumstances?
- How can we formulate our messages differently? Please do this in as detailed a way as possible. Most people have never really learned how to do this.
- Can we clarify our differences of opinion via email, or is a phone call the right choice?
- Should team members address differences of opinion among themselves? When and how should the team leader step in to mediate?
- Which other agreements can help us deal with differences of opinion?

It's actually quite easy: address the issue of how to deal with differences at your very first meeting. That avoids having to address conflict later on. Still, conflict is often inevitable wherever people come together. So who's responsible? People of course, and one person in particular. Who is it?

Become a skilled conflict manager

Team leaders provoke conflict. Of course, they're not aware of it, don't intend or wish to, and often react without thinking. Marie, for example, comments on Jeri's suggestion: "That won't work! It'll only hold us back!" Jeri winces, but doesn't dare say anything. She deposits negative points in the emotional bank account, as management guru Stephen Covey might say. With each one of Marie's unreflected comments, Jeri becomes more frustrated. A couple of telcos later, Marie comes up with a suggestion, at which point Jeri loses patience and snaps back. Marie is livid: "That stupid cow!" Who is she referring to? The person who snapped at her? Or the one who provoked this act of vengeance?

> **Don't complain about squabbling in the team. Learn the principles of non-violent communication (NVC) instead.**

It can be really helpful to follow three basic principles of NVC instead:

- As soon as a difference of opinion hits the table, you have a choice: you can brush it aside and 'feed' the conflict potential. Or, you can take a moment to listen and defuse it. It's your choice.
- An especially elegant way to take the wind out of the sails of particularly argumentative team members is the element of surprise. Team members who disagree are well aware that they disagree, so they expect rejection. Try doing just the opposite and say: "Thank you for your suggestion. That's an important aspect. Let's talk about it." That turns the issue into a conversation instead of a conflict.
- While speaking, keep your eye on the task, but have the person in mind at the same time. Always communicate in a way that lets your counterpart save face!

> **A team is only as good at conflict management as the leader.**

You're not that good at conflict management yet? Congratulations on your self-awareness. Most people don't have a realistic picture of their abilities where conflict is concerned, although most people are familiar with the saying: knowing yourself is the first step towards improvement. The second step is? That's right: practice. Whether you do this auto-didactically or through coaching, the important part is that you keep at it using the tips mentioned above. You don't even have to wait for the next conflict to do it. Those tips work in every conversation. If you apply them consistently, with time and practice it becomes automatic. And the next conflict situation is just around the corner. What then?

Great. A conflict!

There are two types of people: those who feel threatened by conflict, and others who see it as a challenge. What is your take on conflict?

> It's natural to feel some apprehension when you sense a conflict brewing. After the first moment of uncertainty, be sure to tell yourself: I refuse to let myself be dragged down by this negativity. Letting negativity take over gets you nowhere. I prefer to see the opportunities that conflict offers!

Conflict offers opportunities? Who says so? People who deal with conflict. Here are some statements:

- "A good storm clears the air."
- "A good blow up is better than continually tiptoeing around issues."
- "Having weathered the storm together brought us closer as a team."
- "We grow with each conflict."

> Deal with the negative in a conflict (a dentist appointment is worse), and concentrate on finding the 'silver lining'.

There's enough negativity in the world, especially where conflict is rife. We deal with it throughout life in one way or another. So why not focus on the positive instead? In brief:

> Don't shy away from conflict. Learn and grow from it.

You can learn more for your personal development in a single conflict than in five years of business-as-usual. But what good does it do if you deal with conflict constructively and your team continues to bicker and argue? Good question. The answer:

> Whether you intend to or not, or are even aware that you do: when you deal constructively with conflict, you automatically lead by example. In time, other team members will follow your example – as long as you're consistent in your behaviour and give positive feedback when your team members begin to follow your example.

Leading by example is much more effective than repetitive requests: "Hey guys, stop arguing! Let's work together!"

Smoke alarm for the virtual team

Dream teams that run smoothly, have dynamic team spirit, and deliver great results, do exist. How do they do it? By intervening early:

Intervening at the first sign of conflict creates clarity before discord even becomes apparent.

This sounds like common sense. However, it's rarely practised. What happens instead? Generally, we tend to ignore early warning signs, preferring to believe that things will take care of themselves in time: "I don't have the time to deal with this. I've got too much on my plate." That's not a good idea.

***Laissez-faire* is the most detrimental of conflict strategies.**

Indeed, the brewing conflict might blow over on its own – and maybe not. But letting things slide isn't management, it's idleness. And idleness is not what any of us are paid for.

Doing nothing means escalating the conflict unintentionally.

If you don't react when you smell smoke wafting through the house, don't be surprised if the whole house goes up in flames shortly afterwards. Virtual leaders have a keen sense of smell for the least sign of smoke. They are much more sensitive than their conventional counterparts, who run into individual team members on a daily basis at the coffee machine or the water cooler. Even the most cognitive-driven theoretician notices a team member's bad mood. Virtual team members are less likely to pick up on such moods and signals because they so rarely run into each other. That's why virtual champions are attuned to subliminal signs of discord in communication. Read and listen between the lines for warning signals:

- Small talk and informal chatting in meetings, telcos and phone calls ceases. Emails take on a more formal note, participation in the project's virtual chat rooms dwindles, and conversations are noticeably limited to the task at hand.
- Emails and information exchanges are kept to a bare, factual minimum. This often indicates that the conflict is smouldering and well on its way toward undermining productivity. Conflict can flare up at any moment, or go underground to sabotage the entire project.
- Suddenly, the project leader starts to be copied on ccs of email correspondence between two or more team members. Conflict is rife, with team members trying to get the team leader onto their side.
- The frequency of communication between the team members decreases significantly. Emails are ignored, or response times increase. The relationships between colleagues become noticeably cooler.
- Correspondence and phone calls take on a sharper, impatient and annoyed tone: "When are you finally going to deliver?" "What's keeping you?" "I'm still waiting!" No virtual leader worth his salt will fail to pick up on such openly offensive signals!
- Productivity drops visibly, work packages are delivered late, and deadlines are endangered. The symptoms are loud and clear. The damage has been done.
- Rumours run rampant: colleague A has been complaining to colleague B about colleague C.

Is that something you really need to deal with on top of all your other responsibilities? Yes, it is! That's why it's a good idea to watch out for the early warning signs, which requires relatively little effort after a week of acclimatisation. Our attention is ridiculously under-challenged during our average working day. Once you've spent a week paying attention to early warning signs, it will become second nature. Automatic, like changing gears while driving without having to think about it. Just try it!

Take the initiative

Two members on Sven's virtual team have been limiting their email correspondence to the bare minimum for the past two weeks. Both are reluctant to pick up the phone when the other's number pops up on the display. The team has split up into three factions over an important technical issue. As a result, the mood permeating the project has soured. When conflict erupts again, two of the team members approach Sven.

In exasperation, Sven exclaims: "Why didn't you come and see me earlier!" With all due respect, that's nonsense! A team leader doesn't wait for the squabblers to knock on his door. That's not management. Management is about taking initiative, not waiting for a miracle to happen.

> Turn conflict management into an obligation! Make it your obligation to pre-empt conflict between team members!

Yes, I know that means overcoming initial reluctance, but that's true for all worthwhile activities in work and life, isn't it? A marriage proposal involves overcoming one's fears too, doesn't it? Pull yourself together and go for it. You'll gain an invaluable advantage by practising pre-emptive strategies when faced with smaller conflicts during your workday or at home. Tackle the smaller conflicts that you would normally ignore or let slide. It's like riding a roller coaster or hang-gliding: it takes overcoming one's fears and inhibitions, but releases huge doses of adrenalin and endorphins. That's what prompts the champions of conflict management to say things like, "conflicts are fun!" If you approach them proactively.

But aren't mature team members able to deal with their own disagreements? That's a question I hear quite often, and of course, it would be great if that were the case. However, the general character development in the Western world is in a catastrophic state. Just ask any vocational college teacher. It is safe to assume that the average modern human being has only rudimentary conflict management skills. So intervene before conflict causes your team to disintegrate! Team management is conflict management.

Clarify conflict before it gets personal!

All conflicts are initially about content issues. For example, Louis, the technical expert, prefers a steel mounting for the power unit his team is developing. Dolores, the controller, on the other hand, prefers galvanised sheet metal because it's cheaper. Based on your experience of how conflicts develop, what do you think happens next?

> **Conflict degenerates quickly from the content level to the relationship level.**

If conflict isn't nipped in the bud at the content level, it's likely to slowly and dramatically contaminate the relationship. That's when it becomes a big deal! That's why a team leader has to be quick. Very quick. Because sometimes a conflict shifts from the content to the personal within seconds. Take, for example, the situation between Dolores and Louis:

Louis: "With 10 years product lifetime and this price class of the product, our customer expects high-quality steel and not some cheap sheet metal version!"

Dolores: "We've already reached our budget limit!"

(Here comes the shift)

"Why is Controlling is always putting on the brakes?"

Dolores: "Why do you engineers always want stuff that the customer is unwilling to pay for?"

The last two comments have nothing to do with the task at hand. They are purely personal and aim to injure. They cause escalation and kill productivity. Where's the team leader when you need him? Sleeping on the job or just afraid of conflict?

It's particularly embarrassing if a 'normal' team member shows more skill in dealing with conflict than the team leader by taking over leadership or the situation. He might say or mail: "I have three questions for you: what features do comparable products have? What disadvantages does galvanized metal have in terms of maintenance? What is the price difference between both types of metal?" Such questions serve to shift the focus away from the personal and back to the content. You can make this very explicit by shifting to the so-called meta-level, or communication about the communication. For example, you could phone or mail a message saying: "Hey guys, before we jump down each other's throats, shouldn't we first take a close look at the situation? This mud-slinging isn't going to get us very far." So conflict intervention can be done by email? Yes, it's possible, but not advisable:

Conflict clarification via email is a huge mistake!

Why? We've all experienced that: the conflict parties endure an ons-laught of emails, each one leading to more escalation. After what feels like dozens of emails, there's still no prospect of resolution. And even if a solution is finally reached, the atmosphere in the team has turned toxic. Why? Quite simply because written communication leads much more quickly and much more easily to escalation than verbal commu-nication.

Talking to someone face-to-face or over the phone imparts (non)verbal feedback, and you can sense the discord: "Oops, I've overstepped the mark!" This corrective feedback is missing in emails and other forms of written correspondence (letters, reports, minutes, etc.) That is ano-ther reason why virtual teams with weak leadership get in each other's hair with more venom, and are much less productive than conventional teams: they use the wrong kind of medium. They communicate virtual-ly when they should be communicating personally (see in more detail, chapters 10–12).

> If after the third email exchange no solution has been reached, initiate a telco! Or person-to person shuttle diplomacy via telephone.

Nip team tyrants in the bud!

Every team has a top dog, a head teacher, or a know-all who likes to play the role of *ersatz* team leader and hassle colleagues. In conventional teams this sort of behaviour normally happens in team meetings. When it happens, the team leader can step in and put the would-be tyrant in his place. In virtual teams it becomes a problem.

Louis, for instance, sees himself as the specialist *par excellence.* He takes it upon himself to email teammates, asking about and giving unsolicited advice on the progress of their work packages: "You've got to do that differently," or, "Have you completed item x on part y yet?" Understandably, colleagues don't take too kindly to that sort of interference. Their reactions range from mildly shocked to absolutely livid: "Who does he think he is?" But the team leader, Ben, remains oblivious to Louis' antagonistic behaviour because he hasn't been cc'd on these e-mails. That's why, just in case, Ben includes inconspicuous, so-called flash questions in his emails:

> Is there a problem in your team? An undercover tyrant perhaps? You're not sure? Then ask clarifying questions to cast a beam of light on the status quo at the end of an email or phone call, for example. Something like: "And? How satisfied are you with your teamwork otherwise? How is your cooperation going?" If there really is something brewing, these questions are sure to bring some issues out in the open. Once the conflict has been recognised, it can be eradicated.

Well, not eradicated just yet. But at least you're halfway there. The other half is about neutralising the 'tyrant'. That doesn't work with a simple: "Stop that. I'm the project manager in case you've forgotten!" Since you don't have disciplinary authority (see chapter 6), it will only serve to provoke him further. So try a second dimension:

> 'Call off' overly dominant members via pacing & leading. Praise first then lead.

That's what Ben did when he noticed Louis acting up. "Louis, I admire your dedication to the project. It's rare that a team member seems so motivated. You really are ideal for quality control. In fact, you could make even more of a difference if, as of tomorrow, you reported directly to me." The result is that Louis feels flattered (this appreciation is exactly what he was trying to achieve with his comments during the meetings). If Louis doesn't cooperate, Ben can gradually put his foot down more and more. Beware of one common approach that very rarely works:

> **Never criticise would-be tyrants in public!**

That always backfires, and usually provokes acts of revenge and conflict. Deal with tyrants in 1:1 meetings only. In my experience, they realise they have overstepped boundaries once you gently point it out to them.

The goal question

The goal question is one of the best facilitation and conflict management questions there is. Whenever team members start drifting off at a tangent during a telco, meeting or in email exchanges ask the question:

> **"Will this bring us closer to our objective?"**

People like to talk. They like to go off at a tangent and they enjoy arguing (even if they claim they don't). But they also like to reach their goals (because that's what they're paid for, and because we all enjoy success). You can and should remind them of that whenever it makes sense to do so.

> The goal question is even more effective when the team's
> success on the project is linked to a bonus of some kind.
> Then all you have to do in endless discussions or potential
> conflict situations is ask: "Hey people, is this discussion
> bringing us closer to our bonus?"

Unfortunately, many managers fail to provide the right kind of incentive. Again and again, I've experienced managers offering individual team members a bonus if they deliver on or even before the deadline on a time-sensitive project. That's good, isn't it? Doesn't that ensure timely delivery, after all? Well, yes. For the incentivised individual. Not for the others. A bonus offered to individual team members merely serves to erode team effort by creating a culture of 'every man for himself' or worse still, team members try to sabotage their colleagues' efforts in order to secure their own bonus for themselves.

> Individual bonuses erode teams.

The absolute blockbuster is if the team leader appeals to the team members who have no team incentive: "Show some more team spirit, guys!" That approach makes your hair stand on end. People do what they are rewarded for. If lone fighting is rewarded, lone fighting it will be. Offer incentives for team performance instead of incentives for individuals!

Audiatur et altera pars

One day, Ben is cc'd on an email addressed to central procurement and immediately senses conflict potential: "How do you expect us to meet the deadline when everyone in your department is constantly too busy and can't find the time to organise procurement of our prototypes?" In an instant, Ben is on his toes. As project leader, he knows this is his call! He calls the Chief Procurement Officer straight away, who for his part, steps up the pressure in his department. Problem solved? Conflict resolved? Well, yes ... and no.

The problem itself seems to have been resolved, but the conflict has actually escalated. Prompted by their supervisors rebuke, procurement is incensed and quick to fire back: "What do you mean 'constantly too busy' and 'can't find the time'? We were, in fact, very busy during those two days because half the department was participating in a training course, and the other half was in a closed meeting!" Ben had made a fool of himself.

Ben's team member had been under pressure to meet the deadline and, without thinking, had used the emotive terms, 'constantly' and 'can't find the time'. He had not meant to criticise the actual situation. How could Ben have avoided embarrassment and escalation of the conflict? It would have been easy in a conventional team; he could have called a meeting and the staff member in the purchasing department could have clarified the situation swiftly and easily. Virtual teams, on the other hand, aren't able to meet face-to-face, or at least not as often. That's why conflict can escalate much faster. Even the Romans were familiar with this situation when they coined the legal principle:

> *Audiatur et altera pars*: prior to intervening in a virtual conflict, or even when just assessing the situation, always ask the other side first (*altera pars*) how they see it, and above all, what their motives are.

Don't compromise!

Which are the preferred wrong approaches to conflict management?

1. Ignoring, looking the other way, "no time!", "It'll work itself out!"
2. Downplaying, appealing to reason
3. Insulting, commanding
4. Compromise

Wait, why is compromise a wrong approach? So much emphasis is placed on the willingness to work toward compromise! Besides, everyone knows that compromise is always the solution for a conflict. That means that everyone gives way to some extent. And what happens then? Is everybody happy? How often have you actually experienced that?

What happens most often is that everybody makes some concessions and nobody is really satisfied with the end result:

Consensus solutions are better than compromise.

Of course, consensus solutions take more time than compromises. However, everyone is satisfied, which is why they are happy to go along with it (compromise tends to be passively tolerated). Consensus is a win-win while a compromise, by definition, turns everyone into a loser. Furthermore, a shaky compromise has a negative impact on team spirit. Consensus, on the other hand, strengthens it. In the end, reaching a consensus is the most efficient approach. It takes more time in the beginning, but saves time and trouble when it comes to implementing decisions made. Consensus increases productivity. So why do so many marriages fail?

Because, particularly where relationships are concerned, there is a tendency to settle for shaky compromises until one or both partners lose their patience. But that's no argument. In many respects, we're more competent at our jobs than in our relationships. The fact that you can't even make consensus work in a relationship is no excuse. The opposite is true. If things aren't working out at home, they should, at least, work on the job. Otherwise, your income together with your relationship goes down the drain. Turn the scenario around and you might learn from it. A number of project leaders report that their experience with consensus decision-making on the job has had a positive effect on their family life. Try it! Don't settle for a compromise. Instead, take the time to negotiate with the conflicting parties until you reach a consensus. Mostly, it's a question of patience and commitment. What's the difference between compromise and consensus? You'll notice soon enough. Namely, when both you and the conflicting parties are happy with the negotiated results.

Tenderfoot management

Admittedly, you should never use this term out loud! But it hits the nail on the head:

> Every team has highly sensitive members, whose feelings are easily hurt so that they shy away from conflict and internalise their emotions, while quietly resisting progress or even sabotaging the project. Take care of them!

Why? Because they are often particularly important team members or high performers. Even if they aren't ... it only takes one rotten apple in the barrel. One single offended member is enough to herald in performance-killing conflict potential. Therefore:

Offer the overly-sensitive (neurotic, narcissistic, choleric) members of your team more security. Beginning with the first meeting, ideally the kick-off and on a regular basis from then on, announce to the team that maintaining a positive atmosphere in the team is very important to you ('atmosphere' is a signal word for the sensitive): "So, if anything upsets your stomach (signal phrase!), then send me an email or call me and get it off your chest. I'm here to support you. We'll work it out together."

So now you're supposed to mollycoddle the sensitive flowers in your team? You aren't their nursemaid! No, you aren't, but as a virtual leader, you know that quite often the highly sensitive members often have the best suggestions. So, you should be open to what they have to say. You don't have the time? That's just an excuse.

Listening actively to a person whose feelings are easily bruised takes less time the more intensively you manage it.

For example, Shelley calls Ben: "Louis is constantly interfering with my work! He's so mean to me!" Ben is taken aback, thinking: "Oh great, now Shelley is going to pour her heart out to me for hours on end!" And that's exactly what will happen if Ben doesn't take time to give her what she needs.

You'll shorten any conversation faster if you quickly and intensively give your counterpart what he or she needs.

So Ben responds: "You're right, I see your point. We need to do something about Louis interfering with your work. I can imagine you're very upset with him and feel like throwing in the towel in the project. And quite honestly, I can't blame you!" Ok, this reaction is over-exaggerated. But it is just as intensive as Shelley's perception of the situation, and is just the response she is hoping for. Result: catharsis! So after exactly ten seconds, Shelley offers, "Alright, so it wasn't really all that bad. He means well after all ... but I'm glad we talked about it. I feel better after letting off some steam. Thank you!" You're welcome! By the way, in contrast to many of his colleagues, Ben never has problems in getting the best people in the company on his projects. How does he do it? No, this isn't a rhetorical question: what is Ben's secret? What did he just give Shelley?

Right: he offered her empathy. Another one of those loaded terms. Empathy is like penicillin: it works but most people don't understand how it works. Not a week passes without some manager saying to me: "Empathise? What do they think I am ... their nursemaid?" At this point one could start a discussion about how close to extinction our civilisation must be if politeness, respect, humanity, and compassion can be misinterpreted as signs of weakness. Nevertheless:

> There is a causal relationship between a team's success and the team leader's ability to show empathy for members of his team.

So, what is the relationship?

Show empathy!

Why are so many managers unable to show members of their teams, customers, colleagues, or family members empathy? There are two reasons for this.

First, many of us often feel overwhelmed by other people's anxiety and worries. That's why many choose to become managers in the first place: to get away from the shortcomings of humanity. Secondly, because they have heard the rumour that listening actively takes time and that is something none of us have. We can land people on the moon, but we can't listen to Dave's concerns about his work package. That's a sorry state of affairs. But let's move on. The bottom line is that we're all capable of doing better:

> **Even if you aren't on the same page as your team member, empathise!**

Debbie, for example, is a scientist, cerebral and extremely introverted. Nevertheless she has to take charge of a team every now and then. By the time the first milestone rolls around, she is totally perplexed as to why some of the team members are bickering unnecessarily, getting panicky about the upcoming deadline or venting frustration over the phone. She simply doesn't get it. What good does it do? But she knows enough about natural sciences to sense that it would be a mistake to show or say that to her team members.

If one of her team members pours their heart out to her, she doesn't say: "Yes, I understand, I get really upset about things like that too." She can't really do that as she really struggles to empathise with such feelings. But she can show that she's no fool and that she understands what's happening. That's exactly what she does, by saying: "I see that this has really upset you and made you very angry." "Yes, it has," responds the team member. "I knew you'd understand." Debbie definitely doesn't understand. One could call her purely intellectual/mechanical approach mirroring (a communication strategy), but let's not split hairs. The main thing is that the team member feels that Debbie appreciates and understands her, and that productivity doesn't suffer. For that reason alone, every virtual leader should hone their ability to show empathy and understanding on a daily basis. And enjoy the fruits of empathy.

In brief: Dealing with conflict productively

Your project is not progressing as planned? Scan it for latent conflict! Conflicts are performance killers!

- The better the team members know each other, the less likely it is that conflict will arise.
- So, make sure that there's enough opportunity for members to get to know each other (kick-off events, wall of fame, intranet, chat room, etc.).
- Clarify and make sure everyone absolutely understands the guiding principles: goals, goal criteria and responsibility. These contextual factors prevent conflict.
- Agree with your team on the Cohn rule: address disturbances immediately!
- Avoid provoking conflict yourself through unreflected behaviour. Communicate and act in a way that allows team members to maintain face at all times. When nurturing relationships, errors are deadly.
- It's fine to feel momentarily shocked when conflict erupts. Just step back and focus your perception on the opportunities, challenges, and tasks ahead. Like a striker anticipating a penalty kick, it's no good focusing on missing the goal. Instead, zero in on sending the ball flying past the goalkeeper and into the goal.
- Watch out for the 'smoke signals' of impending conflict – and intervene!
- Conflict is a call to action on your part. Don't wait to be asked to intervene!

- Address content conflict before it becomes personal!
- Stop team tyrants by praising them for their outstanding commitment, and then asking them politely to report directly to you.
- If the team starts going off track again, pose the goal question: "Will this bring us any closer to our objective?"
- Whenever you pick up on a conflict on the horizon – *Audiatur et altera pars*. Listen to what the other side has to say before you intervene!
- Strive for consensus. Not compromise!
- Keep your eyes open for particularly sensitive members, acknowledge and listen empathetically to their concerns.
- See conflict as a chance to grow! Learning to manage conflict is a valuable learning experience.

9. Integrate your team!

The elephant in the room

Fritz Perls, the co-founder of Gestalt therapy, coined the saying:

> "One of the most difficult things to see is the obvious."

Put metaphorically, the phenomenon is also known as 'the elephant in the room' that no one sees. What is the 'elephant in the room' for virtual teams? What's your guess?

That's right, it's the distance. When a virtual team project first takes off, there's a lot of discussion about scheduling, financing resources, milestones, goals, goal criteria, responsibility, and work packages. No one mentions that the very next day they will be separated by hundreds, if not thousands of miles. Everyone assumes that distance doesn't really matter, offering lame comments such as: "That's why we have telcos, isn't it?" Hmm: an interesting question. Let's ask Simona what she thinks.

Every Tuesday morning at 9 o'clock, Simona meets the project client in Frankfurt. The project team is developing a new software solution for the navigation of business jets. A large part of the code is being written by her colleagues in New York. The day before, they promised to send in an update on the status of development by early the next morning. When Simona arrives at the office at 8:00 a.m. sharp, there actually is a message in her mailbox. She reads it and finds she has some questions. So she picks up the phone to call New York. No one answers. "Those Americans ... where are they when you need them?" Simona is frustrated. Well, where do you think they are? Yep, you've got it.

Surprisingly few people think of it, and Simona, in the heat of the moment, can't work out that when it's 8:00 a.m. in Frankfurt, it's 2:00 a.m. in New York. So where are 'those Americans' when Simona needs them? They're in bed, as you might have guessed. How many of these avoidable productivity killers have to happen before the team leader finally realises that:

Distance matters!

"I totally forgot about the time difference. I don't know how that could happen," Simona says afterwards. Why wasn't this brought up at the beginning of the project? Because as a rule, virtuality and distance aren't talked about. No one talks about the elephant in the room. It's generally assumed that the question of distance will solve itself. Needless to say, it doesn't:

Manage distance!

With team members based all over the world, integrating as a team is a must if it's to evolve into a working unit. And who's responsible for making this happen? You are: you are the chief integrator. How do you do it? By bridging the distance. Start with a media plan.

Your media plan

How could Simona's dilemma easily have been avoided? Simona did have a telephone list; however, it didn't include the respective time zones. "That should be common knowledge for every member of the team!" is what I occasionally hear. I'm sorry, what are we talking about here? Are we talking about pipe dreams or the real world? Sure, every team leader would like for Simona to 'work this out by herself'. But that's wishful thinking. The reality of it is that team members often overlook 'details' such as different time zones when under pressure to get their work done. The result is hours and days of wasted time, all of which could easily have been avoided by including the details or respective time zones in the list of available means of communication (telephone, video conferencing, intra- and internet, email, snail mail, fax and text messaging …) for everyone to see.

> It's not about the media. Not even the telephone works unless you agree exactly on what medium is to be used for what purpose.

The same day, Simona has another eye-opener. She makes a point of calling New York to, at least, clarify some open questions following the last customer meeting: "Better late than never," she thinks. The developers are tied up in a meeting and can't take her call. An assistant offers to help and promises to relay the questions. A few hours later, answers start coming in via email. Unfortunately, none of them answer any of her questions. Annoyed, Simona picks up the phone to call New York. She finally reaches one of the American developers who says: "Simona, if you need some important information from us, don't call us! As a rule, we don't answer the phone when we're this busy. If we did, we'd never get any work done around here, and our assistant knows too little about what we're doing to pass on the kind of specific questions you ask. In future, just send us an email marked top priority and we'll answer within the hour." Suddenly, the elephant is out of the room, leaving a trail of broken glass behind it.

Simona is furious. Not about the 'damned Americans', but about her team leader: "Why did nobody tell me that earlier?" Well, because her team leader has never drawn up a media plan. He thought it would take care of itself. Everyone knows how to use the phone, right? It would be funny if it weren't so sad: virtual teams are hampered by the most ridiculous obstacles, most of which could be avoided by drawing up a simple media plan to define:

- which medium to use to send information, which medium for decisions, feedback, documentation, conflict clarification, emergencies, deviations from the plan, relationship building and maintenance, personal interaction etc.
- which medium for which counterpart in order to get the desired answers in the form and quality we want.
- what response time for answering via the respective media. For example, answering emails within 24 hours – or at least acknowledging them.
- who can be dependably reached at what time, given the respective time difference (see chapter 7).
- who will update the plan on a regular basis as changes occur.

Why is such a plan rarely drawn up? That's right: because it takes effort. Since when has that been an acceptable excuse? Breathing takes effort too. Another excuse is: "I don't have time!" This usually comes from people who can't spare ten minutes to update the plan, and instead live with the consequences of miscommunication and unavailability of team members. Where is the logic in that? It really doesn't take much effort to create a plan outlining the preferred modes of communication. But for that you need to have understood the investment principle: Invest £1.00 today to reap £1.20 tomorrow. There is, however, another reason why team leaders seldom write up a plan. Can you guess? Who most often fails to draw up a media plan?

It's those team leaders who were previously in charge of conventional teams and who don't even conceive of the idea of a media plan. Beware of force of habit! One of the differences between conventional and virtual teams is the fact that virtual teams need a media plan!

Agree on guidelines!

The developers in New York in the above example tell Simona: "Please send us urgent messages by email and flag them for high priority! We don't answer phone calls!" On the other hand, when Simona calls Italy, Sigi simply says: "Please don't email! We only check them twice a day. Otherwise we'd never get anything done! If you send an email, give us a call so we'll know to check the inbox!" Simona is beside herself: "How am I supposed to remember all that! There have got to be some instructions or guidelines somewhere!" Of course, you'll find such guidelines in the media plan, the most important of which are:

- How we deal with urgent matters … (Via telephone, prioritised emails, a call to announce an email is on its way …).
- Confirm receipt of important news, data or plans immediately upon receipt. Why? So that no time will be lost, and the sender knows that things are on track.

- Agreements made over the phone must be documented in writing by the beneficiary and returned to the counterpart for them to be binding.
- If you reroute your phone to a colleague, not only should the latter be notified (this is often forgotten) but the rest of the team as well, so that colleagues are not put on the spot when they don't recognise someone's name.
- A description of the situation in an email reference line (for example: 'ignition time of the aggregate shifted during testing') is necessary but not sufficient. If you expect or need some kind of reaction from the recipient of the message, then include a clear and polite request such as: "Please send us a readjustment table today!"
- All messages should be as long as necessary but as brief as possible. Some teams actually agree on limiting emails to the length of a computer screen and limiting telephone calls (with the exception of telcos) to ten minutes.
- Send out a status report of individual project areas via Intranet on a daily basis.
- Agree in the team on who will be responsible for both drawing up and updating the communication plan and the guidelines on a regular basis.

Why the last guideline? Well, we're talking about integrating the lone wolves into the team in this chapter. But whoever spends the entire day stewing in his own project package, will remain a lone wolf, in isolation from the rest.

> **Isolation is the opposite of integration; and integration creates motivation.**

Team members who see what is happening around them in the team get the big picture and develop the sense of belonging required for project success. In this respect, conventional teams can learn a lot from their virtual counterparts. Conventional teams, too, benefit from ensuring that their members are well integrated. They are clearly more motivated if they are continually in the loop about the status of individual project steps and there is transparency they can rely on. Invest in clarity and transparency.

The pace of integration

Many team leaders equate team leadership with marriage: after the "I dos" have been spoken, the partner and the marriage itself is largely left to its own devices. That'll work now. Hardly, as evidenced by the divorce rate. The opposite is the case:

It works, if you work it!

Experienced team leaders know that marriages and teams can only succeed if integration happens constantly. "But I can't bring my wife flowers every day!" protests the husband. Team leaders have a similar lament: "How often am I expected to be in contact with my team?" That depends on the pace of integration. How much is enough? There's a simple answer to that question. It depends on the phase of team development (see chapter 5).

- Forming: daily contact between the team leader and the team is reasonable and helpful.
- Storming: when the going gets rough, the team leader's presence is of utmost importance. Once again, that means on a daily basis. The heavier the storming, the more you should use synchronous tools such as telephone, telcos or video conferencing several times a day.

- Norming: depending on how the storming phase was managed, you can start reducing the pace one step at a time.
- Performing: the team leader should be readily accessible, but now rarely needs to be the one to initiate the contact.

Integrating new members into a team poses a special challenge. It's important for the team manager to speak to them more often face to face. If that's not possible because, for example, you are in entirely different locations, nominate a 'buddy': an experienced senior colleague or fellow manager to deputise for you.

By the way, what is the key to integrating people? In one simple word: appreciation.

> Appreciation works wonders when integrating team members.

Incidentally, this also partially takes care of the issue of what to discuss with the team: you'll always find grounds for appreciation. I know, we usually see and address the issues that aren't working. But that too, is merely a force of habit. You can just as easily get in the habit of seeing the good things (too) – and appreciating them. Try it!

> Initially, integrating your team takes some effort but doesn't really require much time. Above all, once you get used to it, it's fun and the feeling grows: my team is fully integrated.

Why is appreciating team members the key to achieving integration? Well, for one, man does not live on bread alone. On the other hand, most people suffer from appreciation deprivation (withheld appreciation). Appreciation motivates and creates a positive atmosphere, which is a phenomenon that we should take a closer look at.

Framing the mood

Let's assume you join the team meeting and the first thing you see is: "Uh-oh, Joe's in a bad mood today!" What do you do? Sure, put on your kid gloves and take particular care to be considerate of his mood so as not to aggravate the situation. You know exactly what's bound to happen if you don't. There will be anger, friction, a poisoned atmosphere and of course, a decrease in productivity. Ok, now consider the virtual team: in a telco, how is anyone going to know that Joe is in an ultra-foul mood?

Virtual teams are more often subject to mood collisions.

Why? Because perception and feedback are missing. As it's difficult to find out what kind of mood your counterpart is in via telephone or email, it's so important to frame the mood to create a positive atmosphere.

A commandment for all virtual contacts: frame a positive mood!

More specifically:

First set the mood, then the task!

Savvy virtual team leaders start virtual interactions with a positive statement, for example some positive news, a project package delivered before the deadline, (rare) praise from the steering committee or the client, a technical breakthrough. Come on, you're bound to come up with something! American team members and managers are well-versed in this art – often they're *too* good at it. A while back, a German engineer complained: "This American cowboy mentality! They spend half an hour making jokes and spreading humour in every video conference. By the time we get around to discussing status issues, there's hardly any time left for our technical questions!" That, of course, is the other extreme: too much good mood. But no one is forcing you to go to the extreme. Find the happy medium.

Disinformation is disintegration

Kirsty complains to the team leader, Mel: "I've just taken over Steve's work package and I've noticed that three of the eight specifications have been changed! Why wasn't I informed earlier?" Sure, because Mel and Steve thought that Kirsty would find out early enough once she took on the package. Or, perhaps Mel and Steve were so busy due to changes in the specifications that they had enough on their plates without having to "inform every Tom, Dick and Harry." Whatever the explanation, it's a dire underestimation of the importance of information:

> Information is integration!

Team members who are not informed react angrily, and engage in conflict (see chapter 8), holding up the entire process. Well-informed team members, on the other hand, are well integrated. They feel part of the whole and behave accordingly. The reverse is also true. People who are insufficiently informed:

- can't do their job due to an objective lack of information.
- feel sidelined and excluded, leading to demotivation: "See what happens if you ignore me!"
- can't just pick up the required information at the water cooler or coffee machine in a virtual team.
- feel uncertain. And uncertainty is poison in virtual teams.

Informing team members too late or insufficiently leads to team disintegration!

"But, as a team leader, you can't really expect me to send out emails and messages whenever a scrap of information pops up!" as I was confronted with by an exasperated team leader. Yes, you can – if you practice keeping your messages short, that is: "Dear all, three of Steve's work packages had to be modified. Sorry guys, it was really unavoidable. The customer insisted on having an additional application. I've attached the details. Let me know if you have any questions." That's short, sweet and integrative. That's how excellent team leaders communicate. Why do so few team leaders master the art?

Because most of us have grown up in conventional teams where the team leader doesn't do much in the way of integrative information dissemination. Because it's not necessary? No: because this necessity is fulfilled in informal horizontal communication, at the water cooler or coffee machine, or simply through the office grapevine. Because of the distances involved in a virtual team, the office grapevine doesn't work. Consequently, the team leader has to take over the office grapevine channel. So start growing the vines!

Avoid a media monoculture!

We all have our preferred mode of communication. Some people prefer to reach for the phone, others instinctively send emails. We all have our preferences. If that were enough, then all we'd need to lead a team would be a list of preferences. That would be nice. However, team leadership does require a bit more competence:

> The choice of medium shouldn't be dependent on your preferences. It should consider the situation and the preferences of your counterpart.

Failing to choose the right medium impacts the overall communication, motivation and integration. Just imagine you send a team member an email and while reading it, he/she thinks of at least five questions to ask about it. Picking up the phone would have been the better choice. Vice versa, many team members complain: "The team leader calls me constantly and talks my ear off. I can hardly keep up with taking notes on everything he wants from me. Can't he just send me an email instead?"

> Be aware of your tendency to a favourite means of communication!

The communication medium you choose depends on the requirements of the situation and its effectiveness in that situation – not on your personal preference:

- An email is a so-called one-way medium: If the recipient has questions, he/she has to sit and twiddle their thumbs while they wait for answers.

- As communication experts have researched, most emails do leave questions unanswered. What do you think? How much communication content does an email provide?? Not many people get it right: in fact, it's a mere seven percent, because there's absolutely no non-verbal communication involved. That's why so many people add smileys and other emoticons to add meaning to their emails. That's futile, naive and hardly effective. A smiley simply cannot replace the facial expression involved in an actual face-to-face encounter.
- Use email only when you wish to inform and can assume that there will be no follow-up questions. Or if they can wait for the answers to any questions that might arise.
- Use two-way channels (telephone, telco, video conference, real-time chatting) whenever you anticipate spontaneous questions from the other end.

These are very basic, almost trivial tips. It's not rocket science. Nevertheless, routine project work is peppered with "cryptic emails from team leaders and members who then disappear on business trips and leave us scratching our heads. The upshot is that the work doesn't get done and we get the blame!" as I constantly hear from team members. That's what disintegration sounds like. Because the right choice of communication medium is such a decisive factor in ensuring performance for (virtual) teams, we'll be taking a closer look in chapters 10 -12.

Management on the fly

Shortly after the turn of the millennium, a German company lost millions of dollars in the construction of a production site in South America. The construction project was managed by a multi-cultural team, and, as is frequently the case where virtual teams are involved, a lot of things went really badly wrong. When it was time for heads to roll, it turned out that the team leader managed the team from the head office in Germany. As one crisis led to the next, he finally decided to fly to South America to see for himself.

He took the next plane, arrived at the site and flew over the huge construction area in a helicopter. The hilarity among those who read the business news was greater than among the management. Because in the management, everyone knew that: "We have neither the time nor the money to be jetting around the world. Besides, we set up virtual teams so that we don't have to constantly deal with organising face time!" These are all legitimate arguments. In a management meeting, the chief controller off a Swiss company described it in a nutshell: "Do you know what plane tickets cost these days?" Whereupon the CEO responded rather poignantly: "And do you know what it costs us if virtual team leaders *don't* travel when they should be travelling?" That's precisely what needs to be considered:

> **If the potential damage exceeds the price of a flight ticket: fly!**

It's not really a viable argument that team leaders stay grounded to save costs. When I consider teams that are in charge of similar projects on similar budgets in similar cost-conscious organisations, I notice that, under the same circumstances, the flight miles aren't dependent on the available budget or organisational politics, but rather on the preferences of the project leader:

> **Travel-happy project leaders travel more frequently; 'desk jockeys' prefer to stay put.**

Which one are you? Don't let your personal preference torpedo your project success! Another reason why many team leaders stay grounded is the common belief that: "Virtual teams save costs!" So we keep team leaders grounded because flying costs money. That's pseudo-logic. Assuming that virtual teams save costs is an expectation, and to date, no one has been able to prove that they actually do.

Trigger management

What really annoys your boss? What does it take to get him to lose his cool? We all know which 'triggers' cause our bosses to lose it. Everyone has at least a dozen or so of such triggers per context. This isn't really an issue in conventional teams.

> If you accidentally activate a teammate's trigger in a conventional team, your *faux-pas* is likely to be written all over your counterpart's face and you can apologise for it immediately. In virtual teams you can neither see it nor can you make up for it immediately.

That's why virtual teams are much more susceptible to hidden and open discord. You unintentionally pull your teammate's trigger in a telco. He or she then sits fuming at their desk afterwards, hundreds of miles away, hating you and venting his/her frustrations on "this bloody project." So what can you do? Some years ago, a very experienced team leader told me her secret:

> We all have our trigger points. Start taking notes and keeping track of which triggers your team members, customers, boss, steering committee members have. Consult your trigger profile cards regularly before you contact the person. It really pays off.

Advanced teams, quite literally, lay their cards on the table, ideally during the kick-off or the first meeting. It can be easily done by posting so called hate cards on the (virtual) pin-board: "What really gets my goat is when I'm cc'd and after having read three pages find out that it doesn't concern me in the least!" "I really don't like it when our marketing people use their jargon or our consultants talk their bullshit buzzword lingo!" These hate cards get people laughing in the short term, and in the long term lead to less conflict, strengthened integration, and more peaceful triggers.

The great integrator

I notice very often that there is a rare breed of team leaders who are adept at integrating their team. What is their secret? They have good people skills, like to travel, and are agile communicators. It seems to come naturally to them. They're simply good at it and enjoy talking to a handful of different team members from day to day. Many others struggle with that, which is why they neglect the integration factor: "It's not my cup of tea! I prefer to stick to the hard facts." I like to ask them:

> How about brushing your teeth? Is that your cup of tea?
> Do you enjoy it?

Probably not, and yet you still do it. That's the point. Never mind fun, some things just have to be done. For example, bridging the distance between virtual teams. Just do it! A little goes a long way and is more help than the lame excuse: "It's just not my cup of tea!" After a half dozen or so serious attempts, you'll see that the more often you do it, the better you get at it and the more fun you'll start having. Especially once you notice that well-integrated teams simply perform better.

In brief: Integrate!

- Distance matters! Manage distance!
- The first step to bridging the distance between virtual teams: draw up a media plan! Agree on guidelines!
- Orientate your integrative team communication according to your team's current development phase.
- Whenever you communicate remember framing: first, create a positive atmosphere, then get down to business.
- Well-informed team members are well-integrated team members!
- Don't choose your communication medium according to your personal preferences. Instead, consider what the given situation calls for!
- It's better to jump on a plane once too often rather than not often enough!
- Start a trigger-profile log for your teammates and distribute hate cards in the team.
- You don't have to be a great communicator. It's enough to improve one day at a time to bridge the distances within the team.

"Just because you know how a phone works, doesn't
mean you know how to use it appropriately."

Frank B., Member of the Board

10. Reach for the phone!

Divorce by text message

Everyone gets angry when word spreads that someone has just ended a relationship via text message. "That's just bad style! It shows absolutely no respect! It's simply not done," are some of the comments people make as they tut and shake their heads, before they get back to work and send off an email to a virtual teammate that drives the unfortunate recipient up the wall. We've already touched upon the topic (see chapter 9), but that's not enough.

Let's face it. We all suffer from email overload. I know managers who receive an average of 500 emails a day! "And half of them have me climbing the walls!" one stressed-out office manager complained. Why? For one simple reason:

The written word can always be misunderstood.

By the way, that includes the wording on this page, for one simple reason:

A text can't respond to your queries.

We know that we can get pretty frustrated when we *receive* emails oursel-ves. When we *send* them we forget about our own annoyance, and justify our own wrong choice of media with excuses like: "These days you can't reach anybody by phone! So I have no choice but to email!" – "It doesn't matter whether I email or phone" – "If I send a half-page email then I can spare myself all the discussion on the phone!" This last excuse exposes the real reason for the daily floods of email:

> People who don't feel like communicating, people who would rather avoid questions, or those who have to deliver bad news and who are not eager to experience and deal with the recipients' reactions: these people resort to email.

Many project managers confess: "Sure, I should really call that team member. But I'll have to bear the brunt of his frustration at the news!"

Emailing is the most elegant way to shut someone down. In other words, you're saying: "I really don't want to hear what you have to say about this or that!" It makes email the perfect medium for cowardly and uncom-municative souls. Many people admit this quite frankly, and I can sym-pathise with them. Who wouldn't? However, it's also exactly the very opposite of leadership, communication, team, social, and every other competence. If, after ten years of marriage, a spouse doesn't feel like tal-king to his/her partner then that's *one* thing. However, if a person at work, as a member of a team or even as part of a virtual team prefers to write emails instead of telephoning, then that is simply a refusal to accept responsibility and an act of self-sabotage:

The opposite of competence is not incompetence, it's cowardice. If you have courage, you won't remain incompetent.

Managers worth their salt are naturally courageous and know the value of authentic communication:

Never communicate delicate matters via email!

The wrong choice of communication medium disintegrates the team (see chapter 9). It leaves team members demotivated and prevents them from asking questions and getting quick answers. But people are difficult to reach by phone these days? Not so with virtual teams. That's exactly why there are guidelines for availability (see chapter 7) and the media plan (see chapter 9). Furthermore, you can send an email in advance and propose a telephone conversation: "I really need to talk to you today. Would you have time between 10 a.m. and 12 a.m. or 3 p.m. and 5 p.m.?" Make sense?

If it does, then you are, I assume, probably at least 30 years old. Because many among the internet generation don't get it. They've entered the job market by now, and they run into serious problems in and with virtual teams. So let's take a brief look at 'what the Internet can't do'.

Cyber-bullying

In both the U.S. and Europe, teenagers have committed suicide as a result of cyber-bullying. In virtual teams, the consequences of the misuse of modern communication technologies are not quite as dire. But, nevertheless, they are bad enough. Why?

Because posting on the internet or sending an email reduces the sender's message to mere text, and that can have dangerous consequences. As early as 1967, Mehrabian and Ferris pointed out in their study, 'Inference of Attitude from Nonverbal Communication in Two Channels' that the impact of communication is reached:

- only seven percent through content
- 38 percent through voice
- 55 percent via body language.

In the case of electronic media, the lack of verbal and non-verbal communication means you are missing 93 percent of the communication that people are accustomed to. The gaps are then filled by attribution and projection. In a face-to-face encounter, the 12-year-old can likely tell by the schoolyard bully's voice and body language that he is really an extremely insecure little brute! If he only reads the posting on the Internet, he projects automatically: "They all hate me! I'm worthless and shouldn't even be alive!" O.k., I'm jumping to conclusions here in order to make a point, which is:

> If you are a child of the internet age who swears by virtual means of communication, then you're heading for a belly flop in your virtual team surer than a novice on a diving board!

Because you'll be posting, messaging, tweeting and sending emails when you should be talking, telephoning or video-conferencing. I have nothing against the Internet. But as Nils Bohr said: "If that's all you can do, then you won't be doing that right either." Ergo:

> Choose your medium wisely!

Especially if it's bad news. Which medium do you think most people, and above all, the grown-up internet kids tend toward? Yep, they send an email. It's so much easier to wriggle out of giving unpleasant news that way without having to face the recipients' immediate response. And we have such people in our teams, or even leading them? *O tempora, o mores*! How would you feel about that?

How do you react when your team leader drops a bad news bomb on you via email? You see? So shouldn't red warning flags pop up when you're about to send off a bad-news email?

Always communicate bad news in person or over the phone.

Whoever doesn't have the guts to do that is a coward – please pardon my directness. The only exceptions are extremely competent communicators. I once received an email from one of my former team leaders: "Dear Gary, I know you wanted to add another follow-up day to the seminar design. I stood up for your suggestion as best I could, but the finance manager stood his ground: it's a no-go. I'm really sorry. I hope you're not too upset." No, I wasn't. The difference was the understanding, sympathetic and charming manner of the rejection. If you can achieve that with similar skill, then an email is ok. So why am I making such a big deal of this?

Who cares how the recipient responds to the mail! "Why should I care if he breaks down in tears after reading it?" is what I once heard from a particularly 'harsh' team leader: "It's about the task at hand, regardless of how the person feels about it!" The underlying belief behind that is that communication is irrelevant! It's the task at hand that matters!

Unfortunately, this belief is fairly widespread in our modern world. It has almost become a dogma. My guess is that you reject this dogma outright. What makes me think that? That's easy: People who lack the instinct for good communication don't read books about team leadership. Your choice of literature identifies you as a member of a leadership elite. Welcome! If we had more of your kind, the world would be a better place.

How we lost the ability to speak

Sensitive issues, bad news: always by phone, telco or video-conference, or better still, meet face-to-face! You'll find that piece of advice in (almost) every guidebook on virtual leadership. What isn't mentioned is that if it's so easy, why does hardly anyone do it? Why are we still dealing with avalanches of emails? Can you guess?

Well, for two reasons: any normal person is simply really afraid of addressing a delicate issue directly in person. I'm no exception, and, I'm sure, neither are you. And secondly, as normal human beings we aren't particularly good at discussing delicate matters. This often has a way of deviating into orgies of self-righteousness, blaming, tirades of justification, endless discussions, relationship issues, conflict (see chapter 8) and kill-the-messenger scenarios. No wonder we all email so much! We think resorting to emails means that we can escape the whole mess. The mess which means: I make a decent living, I have a great job with some influence, a posh car and a savings account, but I'm incapable of communicating bad news without screwing up.

I'm aware that an astonishing number of leaders are perfectly happy with this situation. I'm sure you can think of quite a few colleagues off-hand. I'm assuming you aren't one of them. You would like to see things change, a little bit each day. Am I right? Then the following paragraphs are for you.

How do you communicate delicate issues? In two steps: excessive empathy and an excessively brief message.

What do poor communicators do who have never managed to master their native language? They do exactly the opposite: the more delicate the topic, the more they feel a need to justify being the bearers of bad tidings (the opposite of showing empathy), and the more intensely they launch into a marathon discussion. How about an example?

Marco starts off a telco with: "You are all familiar with the current market situation and the new cost-cutting measures set out by the board (justification). I fought really hard for us (ditto), but there was nothing I could do (ditto). We are looking at another 10% cut in our budget." Bottom line: Four justifications, zero empathy. The telco drowns in his team members' furious uproar. Jennifer's project has also been hit by the cuts.

Jennifer communicates her message differently: "Guys, you're going to hit the roof when you hear this news (empathy). You're going to be furious (ditto). Believe me, I was when I heard it this morning (super empathy: we're in the same boat!). But it doesn't look like we can do anything about it. We've just got to bite the bullet and cut back 10 percent of our budget." This news, too, releases a storm of protest, but it's much less severe than in Marco's case. Most importantly, the rage isn't directed at the team leader! Because:

Empathy reduces the likelihood of attack.

Showing excessive empathy will inhibit a person from 'fighting' back. Or at least, it will keep anger to a minimum and reduce the stress level. In other words:

> Don't placate. It just provokes people even more in delicate situations. Empathy is much more effective.

Let the people get it out of their systems and vent their anger. Avoid saying: "Ok people pull yourselves together now!" That'll just make matters worse. Try showing empathy instead: "I'm as pissed off as you are ...". That's what experts call pacing, and it means going along with or verbally matching the person(s) in question. Won't that lead to endless discussions and whining? No, it won't because the secret is:

Pacing & Leading!

Leading then means stepping back into your leadership position after the verbal matching! That's what leadership is about! Allow your team members to vent their frustration verbally then take back the lead: "I realise this is all really terrible (empathy=pacing). How are we going to solve the problem? How can we make the best of it? What would you suggest? (leading)!" Now you're moving the conversation in the right direction. It's not rocket science, right? Then why isn't it done more often?

Because most managers are not used to communicating like that. They're familiar with the approach, and they claim to understand how it works because they've heard it any number of times in leadership seminars. They *know* it ... but they can't *do* it. Because the fallacy sits too deep: "Once I've *understood* something, then I'm automatically *able* to do it." That's not a misconception, that's megalomania. Not even geniuses are able to do something just because they understand how it works. Stanley Kubrick, one of the most talented film directors of all time, was only able to make such brilliant films because he had even the smallest scenes repeated 40,50,60 times until he was satisfied with the final product:

practice makes perfect. Every manager is familiar with this banal adage, but only a few act on it. Only a few? Yes, and only the best of them!

> Practice makes perfect! Practise pacing & leading every time you communicate in both business and private settings. This will give you the experience you need to communicate bad news succinctly but gently.

By the way, why do inexperienced people justify themselves so much and so intensively when they communicate bad news? What do you think? That's right: you feel compelled to let the recipient know: "Not my fault! I'm not to blame for it!" But the recipient of the bad news doesn't care, because he interprets it as a lack of respect for his own concerns: "Now you've just passed the buck without giving a damn about how I feel about it. The main thing for you is that you don't have to take the blame!"

> Justification escalates, empathy de-escalates.

Obviously it's more comfortable to justify instead of expressing empathy. Unfortunately, comfort-management hasn't been invented yet. Comfort management is not a success skill. Good management and communication skills can be extremely uncomfortable at the beginning. Just like good listening.

Listen!

Thirty-eight percent of the impact of communication (see above) lies in the speaker's tone, not in the content of the message. Anyone who is aware of that will avoid electronic text media where he can. As a Spanish leader of a virtual team said: "If I want to gauge the emotional temperature in my team, I'm not going to achieve that in an email." Because 38 percent of the communication is missing.

In an email response to Antje's suggestion, Derek just types: "Ok, will do." Had Antje called him instead, she would have heard him exhaling deeply just before the ok. Then she could have asked him: "Wait, is that going to be too difficult? Do you have a lot on your plate at the moment?" This would have opened the door to discussing alternative ways and means of getting the job done instead of fixing a date for a delivery deadline, which unfortunately Derek wasn't able to meet. Therefore:

> **Whenever possible, talk to your team members directly via telephone, telco or video-conference. Listen between the lines for the mood in the team, and watch the non-verbal communication. The most important parameters are communicated non-verbally.**

Pay particular attention to changes in the tone of voice, speed, loudness, unusual pauses and breathing. One of electronic media's biggest shortcomings is that problems arising from these missing subliminal cues haven't been taken seriously, much less been solved. It's not acceptable to end a relationship via text message (see above), that is, if you don't want to be perceived as an absolute swine. With regard to relationships, some might regard it as statistically acceptable (plenty more fish in the sea), but a team leader in a virtual team who demonstrates communication indolence on a daily basis? That's team sabotage par excellence.

Listening to you counterpart's tone of voice will provide many more clues to the mood at the other end, the status of integration (see chapter

9), and the level of motivation than if you communicated via electronic means: are there any unspoken questions that need to be answered? Are there objections hiding in the shadows? If so:

Pluck up your courage and address what you think you heard between the lines.

Quite often in seminars managers are quite straightforward in admitting that they have trouble finding the right words to do this. The communication culture in their company simply has no precedent of positive modelling. My suggestion is to adapt a few key expressions as needed to the circumstances and to your tastes. For example:

- "Hmm, it doesn't exactly sound like you're over the moon about that...what's your concern?"
- "I seem to be getting some sceptical undertones. Am I right?"
- "Is there anything else you would like to say?"
- "Hmm, it doesn't sound like you agree completely – may I ask what is bothering you?"

I'm sure the critics among you will voice some clear objections at this point and exclaim: "That's so trivial!" But a large part of virtual leadership development consists of training managers how to talk, because they are often sadly lacking in that area. If you think that's trivial, then I think you're cynical and detached from reality.

Beware of impulsive reactions!

Like with most things in life, you can err on both sides where phone calls (telcos, video-conferencing, face-to-face communication) are concerned, using the medium too little or too much. In practice, too much means too long and too rash. Typing out an email often allows time for reflection while formulating the message. Reaching for the phone is often more spontaneous and impulsive, and words are chosen less carefully. One HR manager recounted the story in a seminar of how she "really put the Romanian supplier in his place" in an emotional outburst. Later she admitted, "I really need to work on stopping and thinking before I pick up the phone when my stress level is up. The people on the other end always seem so shocked." She's got a point, and there's more where that comes from:

- When the heat is on, the impulse to pick up the phone is strongest, and this is exactly the instant to stop and think. Never reach for the phone when you're in emotional overdrive! You'll only drive the temperature up, creating escalation and inefficiency.
- First, get your feet back on the ground, drink a glass of water or go for a walk around the block.
- Unless of course, you are really happy about something. In that case, don't hesitate. Pick up the phone (or type an email instead) and share the positive feedback with your team members.
- What do we think of while we talk? About what we want to say. Sadly, that's not enough. Before and while you communicate, think how the message may come across to your recipient. The tone makes the music, as the saying goes.
- Learn to reformulate your message mindfully to avoid irritation in others. Start off by thinking back to when and where your message caused some irritation.

The irony of that last tip is that those who really get on each other's nerves are often those who regard themselves as rhetorical geniuses. But then that goes for any leadership competencies. To pick up on a concept defined by Carol Dweck: fixed mindset kills! Once I think I've reached perfection, or if I don't believe I can improve, why should I bother any further? I stop working on myself and my skills and fall behind in the process. A growth mindset is the key. I need and would like to hone my skills a little more each day! Also and especially if there are issues in the team.

When there's a storm brewing

Let's connect two key factors of virtual leadership: conflict (see chapter 8) and direct communication (face-to-face, phone call, telco and video-conference). As soon as two people get working on the same goal, differences in approach are bound to cause a certain amount of friction. That's why leaders with weak people skills like to email: to steer clear of the eye of the storm. Or as Antje puts it: "No matter which team member I speak to, after the first two sentences, the differences in expectations are out in the open." So why is Antje afraid of that?

Because, and quite rightly, she is afraid of escalation and conflict! How can she avoid both? You'll remember the elixir we talked about back in chapter 5, and I'm willing to bet you've already tried it out. Remember? Chapter 5, forming. People who are like each other, like each other.

> Emphasising commonalities not only forms the team, it's also a simple and highly effective means of de-escalation, motivation, and increasing acceptance.

Here's another example:
Antje: "I believe we've reached the milestone."
Derek: "But we're still missing the latest test results!"
Attention, potential landmine: open discord and possible conflict on the horizon. However, Antje saves the day.

Antje: "True, the tests are really important (commonality). I agree with you there (ditto). Would it be ok if we discuss the tests after the milestone meeting?"

Derek: "Yes, of course. I was a little worried that you wanted to take the test results off the table."

> If you sense the first signs of a storm brewing, identify and emphasise commonalities. Then ask how you can handle the differences.

Asking questions, by the way, is a helpful cue:

> Many managers make important decisions every day: they're so good at it that they take on a decisive tone even when they're not making decisions. And manage to get on everyone's nerves in the process.

Antje, too, has a tendency to take on a commanding tone in her communication. Derek says about her: "When she talks to us, she always tells us what's what, what needs to be done and what shouldn't be done." She says, for example: "In this phase of the project, when the heat is on, it's better for team members to report back weekly instead of bi-weekly as before." Everyone agrees. Nevertheless, Derek says: "She's like a drill sergeant!" When Antje hears this, she feels frustrated: "That's not how I want to come across!" Well, then maybe she should do what she has heard a thousand times in various leadership training courses and has never really practised:

> Ask don't Tell: 50% parity.

Balance every statement with a question: for example, instead of stating: "As of now, reporting will take place on a weekly basis." Ask: "Should we increase the frequency of our telcos? What do you think?" The tone makes the music, and the tonality determines the integration of the team.

Sure, a lot of managers find it difficult to get used to doing that. But it is something you can and should get used to. It's worth it. Team spirit and performance are likely to improve quicker than otherwise. Besides, we're really not talking about brain surgery, splitting the atom or million-dollar budgets here. We're talking about how you can improve your communication habits. We're talking about words, and whoever is incapable of modifying their choice of words doesn't belong in management. I don't mean you, of course. Anyone who goes to the trouble of reading up on this subject is explicitly interested in improving their skills. Congratulations! That's exactly the point. And by the way, you're in good company, thanks to Marshall B. Rosenberg.

Marshall B. Rosenberg

Marshall B. Rosenberg, an American psychologist, developed the idea of 'non-violent communication' practically single-handedly. I fully recommend you learn it and apply it. It's a great approach. Why not check it out online or get yourself a book on it? What's the basic principle?

It's quite simple: if we aren't immediately understood by our counterpart, we get unconsciously and irrepressibly 'violent'. We get louder, cynical, ironic, sarcastic, snippy, reproachful, because our counterpart is obviously too stupid (this assumption is called the 'mad' strategy) or is just being difficult and/or doesn't 'want to understand' (this assumption is referred to as the 'bad' strategy). We lose our cool, which then, of course, causes our counterpart to lose his/hers too. This is a sure path to escalation and conflict. Rosenberg suggests a simple alternative to this dangerous spiral:

Say what you really mean!

For example, imagine, as so often happens, you say: "It's ten past three already!" to a colleague who has come to a meeting too late. Which response will this elicit? "Sorry, I had an urgent phone call! Couldn't get away!" Whereupon you will probably reply just as impulsively: "If everyone else can manage to get here on time, so can you!" And so, the sparks start to fly. So why not try a different approach? Just say what you really mean, for example: "It's ten past three. I notice it stresses me when you arrive when everyone else is already here. I would like to depend on everyone arriving on time. Could you please be on time for the next meeting?"

Do you notice something? If the message is formulated like that, there is much less of an urge to justify. How come? Because there's a system to it and the system is the system of non-violent communication. Here are the four steps involved:

1.) Speak about facts and observations: "It's ten past three." That's not an accusation, that's simply the time of day.
2.) Bring in some emotional leverage. Emotions move people. For example, (see above): "I notice it stresses me when you arrive late."
3.) Articulate the need behind your statement, that is: "I would like to be able to depend on people arriving on time."
4.) In closing, express your specific request: "Could you please be on time for the next meeting?."

Naturally, there will be situations where it makes sense to follow these 4 steps in your message: facts, feelings, needs, requests. Equally often, the secret is to reflect on which of these 4 aspects of a message you would like to communicate to make your message as clear as possible. This approach is ideal in complex, problematic and stressful situations. Of course, if someone drops something on the floor, you can still say, "Would you mind picking that up?" without fearing the worst. That's a simple scenario. Anything that is more complex, remember Marshall Rosenberg!

In brief: Speak!

- The written word is often misleading.
- Therefore: always convey delicate matters, critical information and bad news in a face-to-face meeting, a personal call, telco or video-conference, never via email.
- Ok, that takes courage. But that's the kind of courage that can be expected from a manager. Besides, it's well worth the effort.
- But such conversations escalate so easily? Not if you resist the impulse to justify your role as the bringer of bad news, and not when you show excessive empathy and keep your message concise.
- Another helpful approach is pacing & leading. Empathise with the recipient's complaining – and then take the lead towards the solution: "How can we make the best of this situation?"
- Whenever you're in conversation with team members (customers, members of the steering committee …), listen between the lines for mood and latent unspoken concerns, and address these issues!
- Never pick up the phone when you are so upset your pulse is racing at 180 beats per minute!
- Discussions during project meetings often escalate. Prevent this in advance by emphasising commonalities.
- Don't just talk. Ask questions. Ideally 50:50.
- Practise non-violent communication (observations, feelings, needs, requests) every day and one step at a time.

"There's no end to all the complaining about the flood
of incoming mails. But no one does anything about it."

Sandra S., team member

11. The email trap

Email guidelines

How long does it take to send an email from Moscow to New York? A few seconds up to a few minutes at the most would be a fair guess. And how long does it take for Geno in New York to answer? Vladislav in Moscow sighs: "It takes him forever!" That's certainly one way to disrupt a team.

> Agree on the team guideline: emails will be answered within 24 hours at the latest. Where this is not possible, a partial, or at least temporary answer is expected.

Why should you spend time on such trivial matters? Because civilisation is in the clutches of a powerful phenomenon: technology is developing at a rate that by far exceeds that of us humans. Ninety percent of the companies that release a flood of emails into the ether have never introduced email etiquette. Everyone fires off emails without thinking about it. And that's precisely why you hear so many people complaining: "I'm drowning in emails!" So here's another guideline:

Anyone who dashes off an email and carelessly or
narcissistically clicks 'reply all' or ccs people who
have nothing to do with the topic is letting the team
down. It simply robs others of valuable time and nerves!

And while we're on the subject of email etiquette:

Keep emails no longer than the length of the screen!

This ideal rule of thumb is consistently ignored. But not as consistently
as if it didn't exist at all! So on we go with more guidelines:

Most emails are cryptic. After reading it, the receiver thinks,
"And now? What do you want me to do?" So, formulate
clear, explicit requests!

Write your need in the subject line: 'Please reply', 'please confirm', 'FYI
(for your information)', 'action required' …

Also, include the subject of your message in the subject line. This avoids
the feedback I often hear from team members: "I often have to scroll
down three paragraphs before I can work out what the topic is!" And:

Remember: do not cc emails that contain criticism or
delicate issues!

That can be extremely demotivating and a burden on the team spirit. Take Dago's example: "The project leader made mincemeat out of me because, admittedly, I screwed up. Ok, I realise I made a mistake and probably deserve it. I can accept the criticism. But not that six other colleagues were on cc. Talk about losing face! And, yes, dear team leader, I will get my own back when the time is right." And so he does. That is how inexperienced team leaders inadvertently provoke conflicts for themselves. Management by masochism.

> The rule 'praise in public, criticise in private' also applies to emails.

Do all these guidelines apply to conventional teams as well? That's right, and they are consistently ignored there, too. The important difference, however, is that in conventional teams you meet often enough informally and can smooth ruffled feathers caused by awkwardly-formulated emails in a personal conversation. In virtual teams, you rarely meet personally. Badly-formulated emails that ignore both common sense and guidelines, create much greater and more cumulative damage. After receiving eight unintentionally rude mails, even the most mild-mannered team member will lose his cool …

Learn to write!

A board member posts an internal memo or writes an email. What are the big three reactions of the average employee? Surprise, amusement, indignation. If we assume that no CEO anywhere in the world wishes to surprise, amuse or cause indignation, then how come it happens? How can that be? Just ask any language teacher – or better still, stay away from language teachers! They're the ones responsible for the mess:

> Written messages can always be misleading. The only difference between messages written by professionals and amateurs is that the pros know they can be misleading.

Vladislav's team leader is no professional, as is evidenced by his email to Vladislav: "The data feed for the range of laboratory tests must be dispatched immediately!" Vladimir reads and understands the message. However, he's not sure he understands what is meant by the term 'immediately'. Is it asap? By today? This week? And if it's really meant to be asap, then what about the top-priority task that Vladislav is working on at the moment? Can or should it be postponed, even though it has top priority? And if so, why can't the team leader explain that in his email? Because he's never learned how. I'll refrain from calling him functionally illiterate, that would be going too far. But I know linguists who would do just that.

Leaders are expected to lead, and as we have learnt sufficiently by now, leadership is 90% communication. Most managers know that but seem unable to translate it into action. That's not an accusation. They have just never learnt how. One thing is for sure: you don't learn clear, unambiguous and effective communication growing up, at school, and especially not at university (just take a look at a dissertation or a master's thesis, or listen to a professor for that matter). So we have to learn it here:

> Don't write emails clearly and concisely; write them so that they are more than clear and more than concise.

Of course your message is clear to you, but that's not the point. The point is: is it clear to the recipient? Ask yourself that question before you hit the 'send' button. Experienced email writers take it a step further. They ask: which parts of the email could the recipient misunderstand? Professionals, assuming they know the recipient's current state and situation, will ask: what could be misunderstood, and given his frame of mind, what will probably be understood? Then they edit and improve the text accordingly. That's how you achieve more clarity, recipient-friendliness and customer orientation.

Writing is a skill that requires constant improvement.

What's the best and fastest way to learn this? Believe it or not, it's by making mistakes. Irritated, Vladislav calls his team leader back and demands to know what the heck he means by 'immediately'. Whereupon the team leader jots down a few notes:

"In future, express exact dates and times quantitavely and politely. Avoid qualitative adjectives!"

Keep a notebook to keep track of mistakes that come up in both your written and oral communication. Refer back to it each week. Professionals do that every day.

Furthermore, it'll help you to avoid the following atrocities.

Email atrocities

"Thank you for sending the scribbles for the campaign so quickly!" Frank writes to Pia after waiting three weeks for the design. Pia is livid: "He can just stick his sarcasm you know where!"

> **Absolute no-goes in emails: irony, sarcasm and cynicism.**

And for good reason: in written form, irony often falls flat. Cynicism and sarcasm can come across as accusations, because the additional non-verbal cues are missing: facial expression and voice intonation. We all know that in theory. So why do we keep making this same mistake? Because, it seems, we can't stop ourselves. Which is why:

> **Even if your fingers are itching to hit the keys, never write an impulsive email!**

You'll only cause damage that you'll regret later. When it's too late. Except:

> **If it's a positive impulse, hit the keys right away (or better still, pick up the phone) before your enthusiasm ebbs and you've missed the opportunity to give positive feedback.**

Understandably, we all get annoyed when some idiot gets on our nerves again. But hitting the keys when you're angry, incensed or disappointed is never a good idea:

> **Communication is not for panic-mongers and amateurs.**

That doesn't mean you should swallow your emotions. It simply means: formulate your message in a way that will help the team. In other words,

not, "Thanks for keeping us in the dark for three days without a word!"
Instead try, "To be honest, I've been a little worried these past days and
wondered why we hadn't heard from you. Do you think we could do
that differently in future?" Clearly, the I-message formulation will be
received better than the sarcastic version. By the way, the best guideline
for emails is: can you guess?

Keep it short!

The aphorist, G.C. Lichtenberg, got it right when he said something like:
"I wrote a long letter because I was too lazy to write a short one." That's
exactly how it comes over to the recipient: lazy, careless, and inconside-
rate of others. In line with this thought, the following also applies:

**When you receive an email containing important data,
information or documents, press the reply button
immediately to thank the receiver straight away and let
him know you received the message!**

Because receivers neglect to respond to the sender immediately, teams all
over the globe spend unnecessary time wondering if their mail was ever received at the other end: "Did my mail get lost somewhere in cyberspace? Did
he read it? Is something unclear?" If, indeed, the mail got lost, something
that happens often enough, then the team loses valuable time while everyone is waiting for the other's response. That's utterly unnecessary.

Always answer emails on the same working day.

It's not always possible? Understandable. What can you do instead? I'm willing to bet you know the answer already:

> **If you can't manage a full response the same day, let the sender know:**

"I'm sorry, I'm unable to give you an answer today – I'll get back to you first thing in the morning!" Or: "I need to check the data and I'll get back to you by 4 p.m. tomorrow at the latest." That stands to reason? The means, yes. The impact? A definite no!

The epitome of triviality

If I may, I'd like to refer to this chapter, as we approach the end, as the epitome of triviality. Reading through it, you find yourself thinking, "He can't be serious. It's so banal it's almost embarrassing!" You don't think so? Then your communication and team skills are well above average because only beginners would consider these ideas trivial.

A professional is familiar with the small differences that make up the big difference. He knows that a few ill-chosen words can cause considerable damage. Just ask any marriage guidance counsellor or couples' therapist. The professional knows that we all know that, theoretically that is. But then … oops, the words are out of your mouth: your spouse is livid and threatens divorce, and your colleague on another continent has made up his mind to tell you to go to hell the next time he receives one of your rude emails, which you had no idea were coming across as rude. Stop doing that. It's trivial and it's irritating. Without a clearly and politely phrased written message, you can't master the four core tasks of virtual team leadership (see chapter 4). The sloppier and more relationship-damaging the correspondence is between team members:

1) the more the subconscious team-feeling (identity) will be undermined.
2) the more team members will move away from each other in order to avoid continual, albeit unintentional irritation (isolation).
3) the further apart the team members feel from each other (distance),
4) and the more difficult it becomes to lead without disciplinary authority.

All this can be avoided by paying attention to email etiquette within the team: little effort, great results. In other words, it's well worth it!

In brief: Get your emails right!

- Agree on a handful of email guidelines with your team under the heading: email etiquette.
- Point out any breaches of etiquette as politely as possible: "Mike, I really appreciate your attention to detail. Please remember, we had agreed that emails shouldn't exceed the length of a laptop screen."
- Don't assume that all your team members are capable of writing emails properly. Help them learn it.
- Do assume that everyone is sensitive about this topic since they often assume that their email writing style merits a Nobel Prize for literature.
- Teach your team (and yourself!) the theoretical background of good communication!

- For example: "Communication can impact our sense of group belonging either positively or negatively; it can bring us closer together or isolate us. It can increase the distance that separates us or bridge that same distance. It's our decision. What does that mean for our daily communication?"
- Make your team aware that a competent writing style when formulating emails is a definite success factor and career booster!

"Our telcos are generally lots of fun.
The trouble is we don't get much done."

Dirk L., team member

12. Effective virtual conferences and web meetings

ꞮꞮ

Telcos on the station platform: Creating context

Making a phone call is an everyday occurrence. But what explanation is there for a manager who dials into a telephone conference from the platform of a busy railway station? What can he contribute to the conference other than a cacophony of background noises? Or participating in a telephone conference while breaking the speed limit on a busy motorway and losing the signal every few minutes?

Technology geeks and nerds never tire of telling us that virtual teams owe not only their success, but their very existence to modern information technology. That must be a slap in the face to any of us who have ever participated in telcos or video-conferences.

Given that face-to-face meetings in normal teams often end up as costly efficiency killers, telcos are the mother of all meeting inefficiencies. Yes, I hear you say, of course there are efficient telephone conferences. I also hear your colleagues' sarcastic mockery in the background as you make that claim. Efficient v/t conferences are the exception and are not part of the problem. We're talking about the others here, so that we can and will solve the problem. So what are the issues?

Is it because once again, technology has surpassed us mere humans? Yes, that's a fair argument. However, you can regain the upper hand by focusing on context instead of trying to control the technology. Where are the individual participants during a telco and what are they doing?

Some dial in while sitting in a taxi or doing their weekend shopping. What's the most bizarre call participation you've ever experienced? In my seminars the participants have so many examples you can fill an evening with them, and a good laugh is had by all. The bizarre contexts people join calls from create distraction, hamper concentration and cause participants to lose focus on the task at hand. You'll hear side conversations with the waiter, the train conductor or the traffic policeman who has pulled them over to the side of the road. Yes, that's distracting and annoying for everyone involved. That is, if they're not already mired in their own bizarre context. So, what can you do? Agree as a team on the guideline:

> **A telco is not a phone call. It's a meeting!**

You don't take part in a meeting while you're buying your breakfast sandwich at the baker's. Then why do so many telco participants insist on multi-tasking on the side, be it via their smart phones, tablets or notebooks? Because they're bored. Well, something can be done about that:

> **Structure your virtual meetings so that participants who aren't directly involved in specific items on the agenda can dial in later or dial out earlier.**

If your team leader is incapable of setting up such guidelines because his narcissist tendencies get the better of him and he insists on keeping his team a captive audience, then at least take the initiative and hit the mute button if you're washing the car or beating out rhythms on your bongo drum on the side.

The triviality paradoxon

I'm willing to bet that quite a few of you are thinking: what? Press the mute button? Don't multi-task? Come on, Gary, how trivial can you get? I got that from Goethe who said: "We humans feel insulted when the most important things are so simple. But then we forget that these things need to be done, and that, on the other hand, is not so simple." Those of us who suffer from the plague of triviality think that just because something appears simple, it'll automatically be done. That's a major misconception. The opposite is the case:

> The most trivial things are mostly left undone, simply because they're so trivial.

Think for a moment of the most trivial; things like healthy eating, regular medical check-ups, enough exercise and no cigarettes. If one of yesteryear's stick-in-the-muds claims, "That's just common sense. Why even mention it?" then just counter with, "Of course that's common sense. But let me ask you: do you do it?" Feeding the cat is also a no-brainer – still, it has to be done. If you find yourself thinking that something is too trivial, remember 'Feed the Cat'.

Doers don't care whether something is trivial or super-complex. They make sure that what needs to be done gets done.

The motto is 'just do it!' Agree on guidelines for telcos and video-conferencing, and make sure that the guidelines are followed. Send friendly messages, reminding members to stick to the agreed terms. Address breaches carefully and politely. Above all: manage virtual conferences professionally. How do you do that? Let's take a closer look.

How to manage virtual conferences

Why is it that even 'normal' meetings get out of hand so often? Because the participants aren't sufficiently trained, and as a result they are undisciplined. Besides, they have such a chronic lack of time in their working day they come to the meeting unprepared. Moreover, the facilitator may not have much idea about professional facilitation but might believe himself to be an absolutely competent facilitator. Then there are the meetings which don't even have a facilitator or chairperson. Everyone has experienced one of those, although they don't dare or don't like to talk about it. Let me break that taboo. I'll take it upon myself to speak out. The relative absurdity and chaos of such virtual meetings and conferences that border on the absurd require it. There is a clear need for a pragmatic remedy.

Designate a chairperson to moderate before every virtual meeting.

It doesn't have to be the team leader. If there's a skilled facilitator in the group who is willing to take on the task, and who is regarded by the team as competent, then the team leader should have the strength of character to delegate the moderator role. What does moderation entail?

Most people will spontaneously respond: "Leading the conference, of course!" No, not quite. It's certainly part of it, but that's not where it starts. The answer is typical of why so many virtual meetings struggle:

If you fail to plan, you plan to fail!

If you don't bother to plan in advance for a virtual conference, then you'd better plan to fail once the meeting is under way. Again, this is common knowledge (triviality paradox, see above). Common knowledge is one thing; putting common knowledge into practice is quite another. There are good reasons for this. What I hear most often is:

- "Sure, I'd like to prepare, but I just don't have the time for it!"
- "A good manager can facilitate a meeting ad hoc!"
- "All the participants are experts in their area. They don't need that!"

What are the most popular excuses in your team? What are your own? In case you don't wish to fall back on these excuses, you might find the following checklist helpful.

Step-by-step: Preparing a virtual conference

☑ Always send a reminder to your participants with the invitation. Phone calls can succeed without preparation. Telephone conferences can't.
☑ Before you send out invitations, ask the existential question! Is a conference the most suitable communication medium? Is it possible to

downscale a little, and make the whole thing smaller, simpler, more efficient and less costly? A regular phone call? A two-way conference? Shuttle diplomacy?

☑ In the same vein: do you just want to inform? Then refrain from following your narcissist centre-stage impulses and send out a mail instead. That'll do the trick just as well and you won't go down in history as hogging the stage.

☑ Virtual conferences are often scheduled far in advance. If, in the meantime, the meeting is no longer necessary, then for heaven's sake cancel it! Yes, I know, that hurts our ego's inner need for self-promotion, but your team will be grateful and thank you for it with a boost in performance. What's more important to you?

☑ Remember time zone differences! Scheduling a telco for four o'clock is an imposition if three team members at the other end of the world have to hang around in the office until eight o'clock in the evening to join in! That's another trivial aspect that's often overlooked.

☑ A tip for the smart people: delegate special tasks! If you are the facilitator in a meeting, somebody else can take the minutes. When facilitating it's helpful to have a deputy (someone who is both sharp and polite) to be the timekeeper and make sure each item on the agenda gets the time allotted to it.

☑ This time discipline can be managed silently, by the way. Just like a referee at a soccer game, you can hold up different coloured cards: yellow means one more minute, red is for time's up, and whistling means you've gone over time. Some teams think it's a great method; others don't like it at all. Choose the tools that work for your team, are appropriate for the task and your own preferences.

☑ Include in the invitation: "Please ensure a quiet background where you will not be disturbed during the telco." Yes, that's trivial, but this trivial reminder improves the chances considerably that people will stick to the rules.

☑ Equally trivial is the recommendation to include in the invitation a reminder to stick to the meeting guidelines you all agreed to at the start of the project.

☑ Important: "One person speaks at a time and as concisely as possible! Please avoid interrupting. We all come well-prepared and bite our tongues when we feel an impulse to launch a verbal attack …"

☑ Ask in the invitation: "Who needs more information on specific items on the agenda?"

☑ Send the invitation early on so that you can consider any feedback.

☑ It's actually trivial, but often overlooked all the same. All participants need to receive the dial-in code on time. That doesn't mean half an hour before the beginning of a telco either. It means several days in advance!

☑ Include in the invitation: "Please have the dial-in code ready." It happens often enough that minutes before the telco is to start, you can't find the blasted code!

☑ Send out a reminder a day before the scheduled meeting: "Please keep in mind, telco at 9 a.m. CET! Have you got your dial-in code handy?"

☑ Another no-brainer: The 'CET' is often omitted when stating the starting time, with the result that people call in an hour too early or too late. Therefore, always add the 'CET' with an exclamation mark!

☑ Be prepared for intercultural facilitation (see chapters 13 and 14). Try to downplay the sometimes-exuberant emotional outbursts of Latin participants; compensate for the polite reserve shown by the Japanese; be considerate of the Indians' strong sense of national pride; and clarify the intent behind the occasionally somewhat dry British humour …

☑ Prepare yourself for the facilitation of culture-specific lines of argumentation. Cultivate the American 'ready, aim, fire' cowboy-style of argumentation with the detail-obsessed style of German engineers, and vice-versa. Clarify comments from Chinese participants if these are characterised more strongly by politeness than by factual argumentation. Underpin the regular 'no problem' comments from Asian participants by asking Western participants to give more details about project implementation. Prepare in advance by jotting down appropriate phrases that might be useful during the conference!

☑ Be sure to facilitate your meetings in a way that allows all members to save face! You don't have to be a Henry Kissinger to do that! You can, however, get in the habit of doing it. So do it please. You'll be doing something for your personal development at the same time that may have a very positive effect on your personal relationships.

☑ Begin with an ice-breaker that you've prepared (see below).

☑ Do you get nervous? That's a good sign. Nervous facilitators are good facilitators because they sense participants' moods better.

☑ You're not in the least bit nervous because you think you can wing it? Careful now! There's a risk involved in getting overly self-confident. The most irritating facilitators are the ones who think they are the greatest.

Mega-long checklist? Ignore the length. Just check the list point for point and don't worry if you have some gaps. The important points are the ones that have a tick in the box. Forget the others.

One more quiz question: which meetings need more preparation: face-to-face or online meetings? That's right. Online meetings need more preparation. Next question: which meetings usually get more preparation? If I ask this question in seminars, the answer is generally, "Face-to-face meetings!" Why? Because online meetings and telcos are vastly underestimated: "It's not really that different from a phone call!" Big mistake!

Step-by-step: Leading a virtual conference

☑ Remember the Big Four (see chapter 2)! Always open a conference with an ice-breaker and/or five minutes of small talk to the tune of, "How are you all? How are things in your neck of the woods? What's new?" Don't jump into the task at hand before you've framed the mood.

☑ Part ice-breaker, part taking the team temperature: "How is the mood at your end of the phone line? How's progress coming on the project? What is the status to date?" Engage in a discussion about the moods (it reduces the perceived distance and keeps isolation at bay).

☑ After five minutes at the latest, move on to the first item on the agenda.

☑ Remind participants at the beginning of a telco of the (not so) obvious: "We can hear each other but we can't see each other." So you can't see the other person's facial expression to know if you've accidentally stepped on his toes. Be sure to express yourself carefully and collegially at all times, and speak up immediately if someone hits the wrong tone!

☑ You can still 'see' your participants: observe their tone of voice, pauses, and verbal signals such as clearing of the throat, hesitation, hmm, ah … These are all signals that let you sense the mood at the other end of the line.

☑ Prick up your ears when you notice particular participants remaining quiet over a longer period of time. What's going on? Ask! But not: "Clive, what's up? Has the cat got your tongue?" Say instead: "Clive, what are your thoughts on that? Could it be that you're not wholly convinced about the idea? What's your concern?"

☑ An ideal way to keep communication mindful and collegial is: ask, don't tell. For example, instead of: "I think that's unrealistic!" say: "What would we need to make it work?"

☑ Asking questions is an art form in itself. Asking: "Are there any more questions at this point?" is a bit silly because you won't usually get an answer. It's a closed question. Unless of course, you really don't want any questions, in which case it's ideal. Open questions are more suitable: "Which questions do you have at this juncture?" That's bound to elicit more responses.

☑ Visualise! That's the top priority in face-to-face meetings and workshops, and works really well in web meetings using the online whiteboard. In telcos, take notes and summarise verbally at regular intervals.

☑ Remind repeatedly but unobtrusively about the goal of the meeting, the project and the individual items on the agenda. Otherwise you risk: out of sight, out of mind …

☑ Facilitate with 'W' questions when you need to finalise the results: "Okay, who will do what by when with which budget?"

☑ Point out every infringement of rules in a friendly but firm manner. Remind participants of the importance of sticking to the agreed guidelines.

This all sounds very reasonable and may come across as trivial. So why don't we experience the points from this checklist in real life? Because quite a few team leaders who chair virtual conferences fall into either one of two extremes: some take a *laissez-faire* approach while others take on the role of dictator. Not because they're incompetent, but because they've done little else in the past 30 years and don't even notice it anymore. We all tend in one *and* the other direction at times. What can you do? Lots:

☑ Recognise your own particular facilitation and communication pathologies. Awareness is the first step toward improvement. Reflect on them after the conference and work on them for next time.

☑ Never try to change things by force: "I've finally got to get out of that habit!" Even before modern neuroscience proved it, it was clear that the brain is not programmed to forget. It can only rewrite old routines with new ones.

☑ Generate new, specific, and constructive behaviour patterns to replace old, repetitive and destructive ones. Go through them in your mind as often as possible (cues: future pace, visualisation. Google more if you like) and practise them whenever you can.

☑ Reward yourself extensively each time you apply the new behaviour, no matter how slight the improvement.

Checklist: At the end of the conference

☑ Summarise all the important points. You'll be surprised how many participants will have already forgotten, missed or misunderstood one or the other decisions made during the conference.

☑ Don't wait until you send out the minutes to include the to-do list. Rather, summarise the who-does-what-by-when actions at the end of the meeting.

☑ Because you're not able to see all participants during a telco, be sure to ask everyone at the end of the session: "How satisfied are you with today's meeting? On a scale of 1-10? What was good? What can we improve on?"

☑ Make a note of the suggested improvements and remind yourself about them in the next conference preparation and invitation!

☑ At the end of the meeting, schedule the date for the next one. It's quicker that way than having to do it later.

☑ An experienced leader is strong enough to break off and reschedule a fruitless conference: "I don't think we're getting anywhere here. I suggest we go back to our desks for now and generate some new ideas that we can discuss at our next meeting."

Checklist: Web meetings

☑ Do a couple of dry runs with the technical equipment and conference software to make sure you know how it works, or ensure one of the participants does.

☑ Familiarise yourself with useful features such as screen sharing, whiteboard, the chat function, how to mute and unmute participants as well as how to hand over the screen control to other participants.

☑ If new conference software has been installed on the laptop, please run a system check and, if possible, a test run at least a week in advance of the scheduled meeting. Every software provider offers a system check on their homepage.

☑ Have a colleague at hand who knows how to work the technology; mishaps occur relatively frequently, are embarrassing, expensive, and avoidable.

☑ Open the online meeting room well in advance to allow participants to log in, and ensure the technology works for them in plenty of time before you start.

☑ Check the height and position of your webcam. People don't want to look up your nose. Request in the invitation that your colleagues also switch their webcams on. Otherwise, you might as well have a telco.

☑ Prefer headsets or external microphones to internal laptop speakers and microphones. Good quality audio is essential.

☑ Ensure good bandwidth to ensure audio quality. If bandwidth is insufficient, switch off the webcam and/or dial in via the phone line if possible.

☑ If you choose to record the web meeting, it goes without saying that you should ensure you should obtain all participants' permission, ideally in advance of the meeting.

☑ Use the available whiteboard for idea-gathering, brainstorming and minute-taking.

☑ Send out documentation in advance and ask participants in the invitation to print it out. In case of technical issues, participants can dial in on the phone line and follow without the screen using the printout.

☑ Agree from the start: whoever wishes to speak, should signal this with a hand gesture to avoid confusion …

☑ Agree on 'thumbs-up' gestures to signal agreement. A general chorus of affirmative mumbling doesn't really go over well in a video-conference …

☑ Web meetings aren't necessarily more efficient or take less time simply because participants can see. On the contrary, experience shows that web meetings take longer than face-to-face meetings.

☑ Suggestion for the kick-off: every participant sends in a picture of him/herself to the project leader prior to the first video-conference. It can then be blended in when the particular participant introduces him/herself, especially if the procurement department hasn't approved a webcam for each participant.

☑ By the way, it makes a better impression all round if the conference leader or moderator is standing during the web meeting – it's more energising and gives the right impression. Remember to set the webcam accordingly.

☑ It is often tricky for the moderator if he's the only one who has a camera and can't see his audience. Another tip from the professionals: stick photos of the participants behind the webcam. In case pictures aren't available, using pictures of smiling business people will do the trick too. You'll feel like you're speaking to a live audience and the effect will be entirely different; more personal connection, more professional, and the meeting will be more efficient.

The overconfidence bias

What's the difference between a successful and a mediocre team leader? The mediocre variety will be irritated by the last three chapters or will just skip over them: "We all know how to make a phone call!" Just look at or listen to a virtual meeting run by a team leader like that. The inefficiency is overwhelming! This is the curse of mediocrity: overconfidence. Really successful team leaders, on the other hand, know:

Communication is everything!

They hone their own and their team's communication skills daily. They are communication fanatics. The result: highly efficient conferences with a great atmosphere with a huge amount of respect for the communication ingenuity of the team leader. I wish you that too.

In brief: Effective virtual conferencing!

- Keep working on improving the efficiency of your virtual-conferencing and web meetings. There's always room for improvement!
- Agree within the team that a telco is not a phone call – it's a meeting! Ergo: no joining from the station platform!
- Preparation is half the battle. Get into the habit of preparing thoroughly.
- Use the checklists in this chapter. Copy and enlarge them; modify them to meet your needs.
- Turn the improvement of conference efficiency into a team effort: "What else can we do to speed up our meetings and get more results?"
- If you find yourself consistently interrupted by the same disturbances: know-alls, the glass-is-half-empty-brigade, egos so big they should have their own postcodes, paranoia addicts, any of whom you may have trouble dealing with (fast enough), ask a professional facilitator, trainer or coach about alternative approaches. Even if there are costs involved, the ROI is worth it.
- Observe and enjoy: the more you develop your conferencing skills, the greater the reward for you and your team; the better your productivity, the more you'll be respected and admired; the more you'll be … et cetera ad infinitum.

13 Leading across cultures

!!

The Babylon effect

We live in the globalisation age. Team members come from all corners of the globe. This is as self-evident as the money that is thrown out of the window in international teams. International teams don't work (there are exceptions), and they destroy more efficiency, year after year, than a global recession could.

How do most board members, managers and those affected react to this? They shrug their shoulders, take it with equanimity and brush it under the carpet. Because the immense waste of money can't be proven in figures (controlling doesn't include the costs of cultural conflicts) everyone pretends it isn't there. Because most managers aren't really able to figure out what the problem is. Even though the explanation is quite simple:

It's not the language barrier that sabotages international teams. Practically everyone speaks English these days. Very few can manage culture ...

Most people don't even notice in their families or their workplaces when their partners or colleagues are upset. With email, telco or a video-conference it doesn't get any easier. This really requires deliberate conscious attention, which often doesn't happen. Instead, the focus is on the task, business-as-usual, individual interests and wishes, power play, cover your ass, institutional narcissism, and making the right impression. That's why few people notice when the Babylon effect destroys team efficiency. People may not even recognise when the Englishman on the team is upset...

All because the German colleague made the frank comment: "That's no good. I can't use that." What in German culture is open, honest, clear, and task-oriented communication comes across to the Brit as a brusque slap in the face: "Interesting attitude," is the Brit's subdued response, which causes the other Brits on the team to smile surreptitiously. From then on, the stage is set: Germany vs. Britain. The score is tied. There's no saying who will win, but it's clear who the losers will be: the project, the company, team performance, the oblivious project leader and everyone else involved. It's horrendous how much money goes down the drain on a daily basis as a result of the Babylon effect.

> **You're in charge of an international team? Good. Do you know how to lead internationally?**

As one exasperated team member put it after an international telco: "That wasn't a meeting. It was a battle of nations." How do most untrained individuals react to such a clash of cultures? With different kinds of cultural blindness:

- Mad strategy: "These damn ... just don't get it!" (Fill in the missing nationality.) People from other cultures are simply, silently and usually unconsciously labelled as 'mad', simple, limited, not as smart as we are, stupid, bizarre, incompetent, strange, uneducated, etc. It's a blinding arrogance that takes away the need to react flexibly to cultural difference.

- Bad strategy: "They're doing that on purpose! They're trying to annoy us! They don't take us seriously! You can't work with these people." They're so 'bad, mean, evil' etc., and yes, that's outrageous paranoia which leaves us thinking, "What's the use in trying to communicate with them? They are just being difficult."
- Denial: "There are no cultural differences in our company." Believe it or not, that's just what many top managers claim. Even worse, they actually believe it.
- Divergence: "Just let them do their thing; we'll keep doing it our way."
- Indolence: "It is what it is. There's nothing you can do about it!"
- Silent boycott: "We'll just let that French guy wait. What, after all, can he do?"
- Indignation and unrealistic expectations on the part of the bosses, CEOs and clients: "They need to learn to get along! They're adults, for heaven's sake!"

As if a certificate in intercultural competence is automatically bestowed on you by your local intercultural representative when you reach adulthood or frequent flyer status. In the real world, however, these types of cultural hostility have disastrous consequences on team performance. Let's take a look at a typical example.

What can we learn from them?

Cultural blindness always backfires, even if those affected are oblivious to it, or if they react to the disastrous consequences with the same blindness as they do to the cultural differences. Here's a typical example.

A Western European team is having considerable difficulty with an Indian team that they hired to take over a number of special tasks. I'm called in to put out the fires. As always in such situations, I ask the European team members: "What do you think you can learn from your Indian team colleagues?" As usual, I get the same response to this question.

There is a lot that can be learned from Indian team members. They are more easy-going, are extremely competent multi-taskers and incredibly tolerant of ambiguity and uncertainty. In these respects and others, they could be great role models. But that doesn't happen. When I ask what the Western European team could learn from their Indian colleagues, they look taken aback by the question. After a long silence and some very thoughtful expressions, one member of the team speaks up: "That's a good question. We've never really considered that. To be honest, we're not really interested in learning anything from them!" Why not? What's your idea? What does your intercultural competence tell you?

You've got it: "We're not really interested in learning anything from them. We hired them because they're cheap!" Wow. That sort of attitude in the age of globalisation. When the European team finally understands why there is so much friction between them and the Indian colleagues, the team leader exclaims in mild shock: "For the past weeks now we've been trying to improve efficiency in the team, and now, when we have the ideal chance to learn something, we ignore it out of pure arrogance. Great. I feel really embarrassed …" At least the man realised the situation in time. A lot of people never work it out.

Instead of fleeing from cultural blindness in all its forms (see above) and bearing the ensuing conflicts, one could simply ask:

> "They do things quite differently. What could we learn from them?"

Why is this simple question asked so rarely? Because we are looking through our own cultural glasses. And with these glasses we judge instinctively ethnocentrically: "What are they doing? That's wrong!" Once you become aware of these hasty judgements and resist the temptation to fall for them, you've attained intercultural competence.

Another example: after a meeting, a manager complains: "My negotiation partner didn't shake hands with me when we met at the meeting. I think he may have a problem with me!" As a matter of routine, I usually respond: "Where was he from?" Our cultural glasses make us assume so many similarities that just aren't there. If we miss a ritual like a handshake, because in our counterpart's culture it is much less usual, it makes us reach all kinds of wrong conclusions.

Or, in another case: a Western manager sees two men crossing the street holding hands. His first association is spontaneous and clear. And incorrect. He sees the men in Riyadh and not somewhere in the western world. In London, for instance, this gesture has an entirely different connotation than in Riyadh. Only, many westerners don't realise this. They realise they're physically in Riyadh, but they're not aware that they're still in the mindset of their home culture. Of course, every international jet-setting businessman knows from countless intercultural training courses the importance of being open-minded. Just about every intercultural trainer makes this point during the first hour of an intercultural awareness seminar. The participants nod vigorously, as this is very helpful advice. Not for themselves of course. But for the other participants in the room.

No frequent flyer executive has ever folded his hands on his head in a eureka moment at this juncture in the training course and said: "Thank you! Oh my God! Until now I have been so close-minded!" That doesn't mean he hasn't been. He just lacks cultural self-awareness and merrily travels the world asserting his way of doing things on his global team, justifying his dominant dogma by calling it 'corporate best practice'. More often than not, the project is successful, but the collateral damage in cultural trust-building is immense. Which is why so many managers wonder about the high levels of fluctuation. As one senior executive put it: "These people are so disloyal."

> **What is the first thing you should think when you encounter the signals indicative of a culture other than your own?**

There's only one answer to that question, and it consists of just one word. Do you know it? Are you globalisation-competent? The answer is: "Interesting!" That's what a professional thinks when he encounters an unfamiliar culture; one hundred times an hour, and at night in his dreams. Are you feeling out of your element with this topic? Not to worry, you're in good company.

Intercultural meta-communication

Sure, any reasonable individual would rather give this topic a wide berth. Many team leaders almost pleadingly ask me: "Do we really have to address these issues? I mean, we travel extensively and have spent a lot of time on business or on holiday in other countries. We're familiar with their way of life, and the differences aren't all that great." My guess is that if you didn't know the answer, you wouldn't be here. The answer lies in these three words: yes, yes, and yes.

- Address 'interculturality'! At the kick-off or at your first team meeting.
- Reserve at least an hour of your time to do this. Believe me, you'll need that hour.

- Some teams bring in a competent cross-cultural trainer to address the issue.
- It's even more effective if team members or members of the respective countries on the team discuss their different approaches: "How do we communicate in the culture I come from? How do we give instructions and feedback? What is our understanding of punctuality, quality …?"
- Helpful hint: inform yourself about intercultural dos & don'ts, especially where communication is concerned.
- Important: do's & don'ts aren't really helpful if the corresponding intercultural awareness is missing. Therefore: develop your awareness, for example, with case studies like the one that you have just read (see above).
- If you have (anonymous) real-life case studies taken from incidents that occurred in earlier projects to practise and role-play with, that's best of all.
- For the more advanced: address typical stereotypes with sensitivity and humour. For example: "In our culture we think you Spaniards are fiery, loud and always late. I'm sure you see that differently, right?" If you have a good understanding on the relationship level, it's easy to address and dispel prejudices by talking about them.
- No money or no time for a decent cross-cultural briefing? That's hard to believe. You do have a project budget, right? So redistribute some of your funds. Cross-cultural training is one of the best investments you can make. It pays off. It's the best preventative measure to avoid future costs caused by conflict, loss of efficiency, friction...
- Set up a forum on your inter-/intranet to address cross-cultural issues, questions and feedback.
- Make understanding and constructive feedback one of your top priorities in the team.
- That means that colleagues give each other the benefit of the doubt if someone should inadvertently breach cultural etiquette.

- At the same time, your commitment to giving each other feed-back allows and expects you to gently remind each other of in-tercultural *faux pas* and to offer each other advice on how things could be done more mindfully.

It would be fair to assume that every reasonable team is able to practise these tips. But as we know all too well, the trouble with common sense is that it's not all that common. Following the list above could save quite a few headaches, and avoid three of the most common consequences:

- Cultural egocentrism
- The chameleon effect
- Cultural stalemate.

Let's take a look at these three battleground scenes, one at a time.

Cultural egocentrism

The British engineer is sitting at the bar in New York with his (predo-minantly) British colleagues: "You can't even get a decent pint in this place. Haven't they got a proper pint of bitter? You can't drink this stuff." What's happening here?

That's the caveman abroad – the most frequently occurring *faux pas*. Everyone has run in to them at one time or another. No one is immune – myself included (maybe not as extreme when it comes to beer). But that's not the point. Rather:

> You are bound to commit one or another cultural *faux pas* unintentionally. What's important is that you notice it, apologise, correct it immediately, and make sure it never happens again.

That's exactly what cultural egocentrics don't do – they just repeat the same Neanderthal grunts: "These …! (fill in the missing nationality), someone should teach them … (fill in virtue, skill, competence)!" At this very moment, many German managers are trying to teach Chinese employees what is meant by German punctuality. The cultural egocentric doesn't understand what he's doing wrong. The more culturally aware in the group despair, while the Chinese employee feels insulted, to say the least. That's life, I hear you say? Well, it's not as simple as that. Convince yourself:

Have you ever noticed how unpopular 'the Americans' are in Arab cultures? Though not intending to provoke, without realising it, they act as if theirs is the dominant culture regardless of where they are in the world. In the West this is often laughed about. To the Arabs, however, it's a deadly insult. In every sense of the word. When the allied forces occupied Iraq, the British and American troops tried to stem the tide of ongoing terrorist attacks by increasing roadside patrols. The British had far fewer incidents, shootings and casualties on their patrols. How come? There were many reasons, a lot of which were culturally based. One central reason was: Americans patrolled wearing helmets and sun glasses, and, for the most part, neglected to greet the people they stopped. The Brits on the other hand, politely removed their sunglasses and greeted the people, as often as they could, in the native language. The Brits were polite to the people and respectful of the culture. As a result, they experienced less aggression. Once one has looked the other person in the eye, and that person greets politely in one's native language, the impulse to react aggressively is greatly diminished:

Cultural egocentrism can have life-threatening consequences. The fact that it happens unconsciously doesn't bring the dead back to life …

That makes sense. Why don't more team leaders intervene when members commit cultural *faux pas* unintentionally? Because they are stuck in task focus: "But the Indians agreed to deliver the work packages yesterday, yet they still haven't delivered! Someone should bring them into line!" Some people never learn.

'Bringing them in line' doesn't work interculturally. Not even if you're dealing with the most disciplined people. You can tell an Indian that he's doing a great job, but that 'our clients' here in the West are sometimes a bit strange. Not only do they fail to appreciate that you will deliver on time, but, in addition, they want you to follow the milestone plan exactly to the date and time. Can you believe that? "I mean, I wouldn't mind," as an interculturally competent team leader explained to his Indian supplier, "but I'll lose face with my boss if we don't stick exactly to the plan." Put that way, the Indian was able to understand the situation immediately. Saving face. Under no circumstances could he allow his Western European client to lose face with his manager like that. Since then, work packages have been noticeably more punctual. That's the secret:

> Look beyond your own cultural perspective. Find out what's important to your counterpart and argue from his perspective. Even if it seems strange, absurd and exotic to you. Logic won't help. Cultural intelligence will.

An HR executive at an IT company once asked me: "How can I drive the cultural egocentric out of a German professional in the chemical industry who for the past 30 years has believed that German chemical experts are the best in the world, and is convinced that the Brazilian colleagues are quacks?" My response: "Not by giving him a crash course." Moderate egocentrics can be cured by repeatedly calling their attention to cultural awareness and by having a team leader who reminds them on a regular basis. In the case of incurable egocentrics, there's only one solution: keep them out of international teams! It's better to bring in the second-best specialist. What he lacks in expertise, he'll make up for in cultural competence.

For all of those in the middle, there's Ruth Cohn's maxim: "Address any discord immediately!" The more often the team leader reminds members of this adage, and the more often the team members point out to the egocentric that even though he probably didn't mean it the way it came across he might want to reformulate his remark, the sooner the cultural penny will drop for the egocentric. He's likely to realise that, in fact, he didn't intend his message to injure or insult. Thanks to the other members' gentle reminders, he'll probably choose his words more carefully the next time. Egocentricity is not a terminal disease: cultural egocentricity can be cured. A cure that is well worth the effort.

Once you've achieved cultural competence, your international partners and team members will begin to respect, even cherish you. That's what people tend to do when they feel well-treated for a change. And your reward: team performance improves immensely.

The chameleon effect

Cultural egocentrism is bad. But to slip to the other extreme is no solution either. Of course, as a Norwegian, you should be able and willing to join in an intranet discussion with the two Italian members on the team on the best recipe for pizza. But it makes no sense for a Swiss national to join in with the Italians in complaining about the mafia and the incumbent Italian government. Especially because you shouldn't relinquish the strengths of your own culture without good cause either.

Treat other cultures with respect, but there's no need to 'go native'! Assimilation is not a gesture of respect. If a Spanish businesswoman suddenly turns up at a business meeting in Tokyo in a kimono, all those present will grimace in embarrassment. That's not showing respect, that's ingratiation. That kind of invasiveness is often misinterpreted as presumptuousness. It's perfectly ok to show allegiance to your own culture. After an initial attack of outright cultural egocentrism, the French team leader, for example, never called a meeting or telco during Friday prayer time. The three Muslims on his team appreciated that – but they'd be utterly astonished if the team leader suddenly appeared in their midst at a mosque. The same goes for business dinners.

When a dyed-in-the-wool Englishman visited the Texan heartland, he was actually served shepherd's pie, to remind him of home. The Englishman commented dryly: "I was just there for a quick visit and would be back home within three days. Besides, no one in America makes shepherd's pie like my mum! And to top it all, I really would have really enjoyed an authentic Texan barbecue – that's something I can't get in Manchester!"

> Respect and appreciate other cultures. Don't bend over backwards to conform. That's a different form of lack of respect.

Cultural stalemate

Since so much has been done wrong since the invention of globalisation, this has led to a lot of intercultural headaches in many teams and companies. In one medium-sized company everyone who joins the team knows to: "Watch out for the Spaniards, they have their siesta from 11 a.m. to three in the afternoon!" The Spaniards, for their part, whisper:

"Just ignore the German hair-splitters. Their bark is worse than their bite." Whenever a German-Spanish project is in the pipeline, the CEO sprouts a few more grey hairs: "The projects are outrageously ineffici-ent." Why?

Because they've reached a cultural stalemate: everyone is aware of it, but no one does anything about it. Except for Moral Suasion: "Guys! Pull yourselves together! Things have got to change." They won't. Not unless someone works out how to break the stalemate:

> **A stalemate doesn't resolve itself, not even through appeals or divine intervention. It can only be resolved through mediation.**

How? The easiest way is to hold a kick-off. Once people get to know each other personally and establish working relationships, they're less likely to attack each other. They treat each other with respect and overcome cultural barriers. If you haven't got the budget for a kick-off, then you can always resort to mediation in the classic sense. Schedule a meeting or telco to discuss the issue of 'cultural conflict'. "I'm not competent in that area," is not an argument that holds water.

All you need is some courage and lots of common sense. Of course, you can also hire an external intercultural mediator with conflict and cultural competence if you have the budget for it. If he's worth his salt, he won't go into the reasons for the stalemate. Instead, he'll come to the point once everyone has had a chance to vent their feelings and frustrations. What needs to change about the way you treat each other, the way you com-municate, and the processes that are currently in use, so that you can get along better together in future? Then you initiate a brainstorming session, and agree as a team on what can be done. And bingo! The stalemate begins to dissolve. Sure, there'll be some grumblings along the way, but grumblings are better than stagnation. What do high-performance teams do?

The best of all worlds

If it weren't for the occasional dream team, it would be easy to lose faith all together. High-performing teams have managed the cultural issue as only high-performing teams can: there is no single lead culture, or one culture that dominates over others.

Instead, there is a team culture that includes selected elements of individual national cultures. As a project leader in the cosmetic industry told me once: "It's actually a lot of fun, and it's useful to boot. When we analyse lab results we pursue the precision of the Swiss colleagues. But where processes and consensus are concerned we look to our Italian contingency: lots of back and forth discussion, laughter and helping each other out when the going gets tough. Things may go wrong from time to time, but no one gets in a tizzy about it, and everyone lends a helping hand to work it out." After a moment of reflection, she adds: "I wish my family life were half as harmonious." Hmm, what can one say to that? Apparently team competence not only makes you a better team leader, but is also good for your family life, if you give it a chance.

The language barrier

A German company buys a company in Romania. None of the managers of the German company speak Romanian; none of the managers of the Romanian company speak German. In spite of this, meetings are held without the support of an interpreter: "We all speak English after all," says the German CEO." "What they call spoken English is a disaster," say the German managers at the negotiation table. No one knows what their Romanian counterparts have to say about that because no one speaks their language. The company was bought up cheap (the only way companies are snapped up) because it was in trouble. The German company was determined to turn the company around within six months to secure the credit line. A year later, the losses are piling up. The bank has become impatient, and ominous signs of a cultural stalemate are starting to appear (see above) …

When the focus is solely on market opportunities, prestige, investment opportunities and cash flow, the language barrier is mostly either overlooked or ignored.

When this problem comes to light and I ask how come interpreters haven't been brought in, the response is often: "We thought that with time we'd be able to manage without!" That's insane. There's only one solution:

Overcome the language barrier!

- Clarify what the official language in the team should be.
- If it's to be English, make sure that everyone really does speak the language!
- Try to find this out beforehand.
- Do it gently. Very few people will openly admit their Anglophobia or poor knowledge of English.
- In long-term projects, organise language courses! That's always worth it.
- Do it as conveniently as possible: blended learning is optimal for sustainability; e-learning is the minimum.

- Ask HR or Training & Development why, with so many international projects, language courses aren't more compact and more easily accessible.
- Establish the maxim that making fun of a colleague's language ability "does nobody any favours!"
- Explain: "If something isn't clear, ask! Usually, it has nothing to do with the task at hand or a colleague – it's usually the language!"
- Agree: "If something isn't clear due to a language issue, please ask for clarification immediately."
- And: "No smirking to yourself surreptitiously if someone asks for clarification of a language question."
- Adapt to your counterpart's language level. If you're a native speaker, your colleagues who are not may need a helping hand. Cut out the slang, slow yourself down and simplify your choice of words. Give them a break!
- Never make fun of your colleagues' linguistic proficiency! That's really bad style, and remember, 'What goes around comes around'.
- When language competence is not as good as it could be and gets in the way of clear communication, try a simplified form of Marshall B. Rosenberg's approach (see chapter 10). It's better than spending all your precious free time learning vocabulary: 1) facts, observations, 2) feelings, 3) needs, 4) requests. Remember: if the thinking is clear, the language will follow suit and come across more clearly.
- General tip: The less you understand the language, the more intensively you should employ a method called controlled dialogue. That means: repeating what your counterpart said to ensure you've understood, paraphrasing, asking clarifying questions, summarising, and asking for confirmation. It works really well in one's own language too.

The annoying thing is not the language barrier as such; it's the fact that it's the elephant in the room that nobody is addressing! But I'm preaching to the converted: you are here, which means you're interested in developing your skills. Don't worry. You'll do it better.

How much directness is acceptable?

It's not enough to master a language. You also need to understand the difference between direct and indirect communication styles.

Which nationalities often like to get to the point immediately without beating about the bush? That's right: the Dutch and the Germans. "No, that's not how you do it!" You'll hear this in both countries on a daily basis. Not so in China, India or other Asian countries, nor indeed in England. In these countries the communication style is more indirect. Why? Time for a small test of your intercultural competence.

That's right, you've got it: because indirect communication in cultures that communicate indirectly serves to protect the relationship. Because an outright 'no' or a refusal or a rejection may lead to loss of face. That's one reason why Indians often don't say 'no', for example. They say no by saying yes and packaging their no in such a way that people from many other cultures have a hard time deciphering the no behind it. With a little intercultural competence this becomes easier to recognise. Generally speaking, Indians will answer in the affirmative to most suggestions. If, by chance they don't, or the yes is preceded or succeeded by a pause or hesitation, it's cause enough to stop and think, because then it's usually an Indian 'no'.

- Address the issue of country-specific use of language using formulations directly related to your project. For example: "If our South Korean colleague says, 'no problem, we'll do it right away,' it means …"

- Translate indirect wording into direct language. If, for example, an Indian says, "I'll try!" then that's a very elegant, culturally-based way of saying 'no'.

- Create a 'direct-indirect' dictionary so direct speakers can learn to formulate their messages more indirectly, and can translate indirect phrases and formulations into plain, direct language. Indirect language speakers learn to avoid misinterpretation: they learn that direct speakers don't mean it personally and don't consciously intend to offend.

- Include basic translation guidelines: "Don't just take the words you hear at face value, but 'read the air': look for and listen for meaning between the lines!" That means the whole context, including voice nuancing, hesitation, and body language (if observable).

- In case the meaning is even slightly unclear: clarify. The standard questions here are: "In my culture that would mean ... Is that what you are saying?" or "What exactly do you mean by that? Wie meinen Sie das? Qu'est-ce que ca veut dire?"

Smart communicators communicate carefully; that means, in full awareness of their own use of language. For example, after a 5-minute outburst of passionate enthusiasm embellished with colourful superlatives about the current project status in a video conference, an Italian engineer added as an afterthought: "Or as my German colleagues would say: 'Everything is going to plan.'" One of the German team members responded in the same vein shortly after with a mischievous wink and accompanied by the laughter of the rest of the team: "Those were the figures. If I were Italian, I'd say: these fabulous results add to our 'bella figura'!" That's intercultural competence. The positive mood in this team is palpable; it is evident that everyone enjoys working there. When work is enjoyable, the quality of the work improves. Please keep that little nugget of management wisdom to yourself, it's a secret....

Deep in the Middle Ages

Susanne is beside herself: "These Slovenians! They promise the Earth, but don't deliver. The milestone results were due yesterday morning at the latest and today there's still no news! I'm going to give them a piece of my mind!" Gabi has a little more intercultural competence, and stops her from doing so with some good advice: "Why don't you check if the report got stuck somewhere before you jump in their faces?" Susanne takes her advice.

As it turns out, the CEO had seized the milestone results to present as Good News at his upcoming meeting at Head Office. On hearing this, Susanne exclaims: "Just imagine if I had snapped at Slovenians! The next milestone would never have come in on time: they would have had their revenge. They are only human after all."

> Prejudices kill competence.

As homo sapiens, we are all susceptible to prejudices (myself included). That's our evolutionary heritage and we are more or less condemned to live with it. It becomes a problem if we allow subconscious prejudices to sabotage work, performance and reputation. Gabi is aware of this, and intervenes whenever she senses that there are prejudices at work.

> Whenever prejudices crop up within the team, even if they are meant as a joke: intervene! Do it patiently and carefully, but be absolutely resolute.

In mediocre and badly-run sales teams, for instance, guess what topics of conversation circulate? Right: conversations involving prejudices about customers. "These people have no idea how the technology works!" Of course, they can find enough 'evidence' to substantiate such prejudices. But what good does it do? You'll never hear comments like that in high-performance teams. What you do hear is something to the tune of: "The customer doesn't seem to have grasped it yet? What do we need to change in the way we communicate for them to understand what we mean?" Top performers don't focus on prejudices; they focus on solving problems. But that too, is a question of personal preference: which of the two do you prefer?

When the house is on fire: don't panic!

Werner calls Vienna from Mexico: "Can you imagine, our first business meeting was scheduled for yesterday, and they had nothing better to do than invite me to a party! I don't think we can do business with them. It's obvious they're not taking our offer seriously!" That's a tricky situation; we're talking about a €400,000 order here. Not exactly peanuts for his regional Austrian operation. What should Werner do? Break off negotiations? Werner's boss, the CEO of the company back in Austria, is just as clueless: "But they led us to believe that this deal was important to them! What's the matter with these Mexicans?"

That's exactly the problem (see above): prejudgement. Prejudgement is always harmful. In delicate situations it's lethal. Luckily, Werner got on the phone to an old friend, a journalist from Mexico, and told him about this experience. "You fool!" was the response he got. "That was a real honour! In that region the 'party' you mention is something akin to a national holiday! Normally, no gringos are invited to such an exclusive event! Get back to the Mexican first thing in the morning and thank him for the invitation! It sounds like they are really keen to work with you!"

- In delicate situations, switch off prejudgement and fine-tune your perception. Then observe what is happening really closely: what is being said and done? What happened before the situation?
- Avoid spontaneous reactions and jumping to conclusions! Delay judgement until you can get more information! Ask someone who is familiar with the culture before you do something you'll regret.
- Keep your contacts network up to date: for every culture you work with, it helps to know someone whose advice you can trust. (Refer to Google as a last resort!)
- Humour, humility, patience, appreciation, flexibility and a sincere interest in the other are not only noble characteristics; they also help you to cope in a cultural crisis. Don't worry, with practice, these characteristics can be developed …

The advanced level

There is a thin line between cultural behaviour and individual behaviour, as the following example demonstrates.

Brenda hosts a visit from a Turkish colleague. After they have finished work and settled business issues, Brenda invites him to dinner. He declines, whereupon she says: "Oh, come on, it'll be fun." He declines a second time, and Brenda gives up.

The following day, his day of departure, she expresses her regret that they didn't go out for dinner. He says: "I would have liked to join you, but you should have asked me more times. Then I would have come." Brenda is flabbergasted. It feels like a declaration of bankruptcy of her intercultural competence.

She asks a Turkish colleague: "I thought I was familiar with Turkish customs. Is that really the case? Or is it generally not acceptable for a woman to invite a Turkish man to dinner?" The colleague blusters: "What do you take us for? We're not country bumpkins, you know. Of course, a woman can invite a man to dinner. And of course there are still some regions where people maintain the custom that a guest must be invited several times to show the sincerity of the invitation. But in Ankara or Istanbul, we don't go by that tradition any more. If you ask me, I'd say your Turkish colleague has a screw loose." Does that help Brenda?

Yes, it does. Brenda's intercultural/interpersonal skills are enviably well-developed. She responds: "If a colleague chooses to adhere to the customs of his country, even if they aren't adhered to in the cities or more modern regions of the country, it is still his custom. It would be stupid to ignore that." So she sends him a mail informing him that she has been able to locate an under-the-counter version of an old Kirk Douglas film that he had expressed an interest in but was unable to find. She asks if he is still interested. He declines. Two days later she offers to send the DVD again and again he declines. Three weeks later, after offering several times, he writes that he is delighted and accepts. Pam sends out the DVD with her best regards. Two months later, a key Turkish supplier defaults on a delivery. Not even an intervention by the managing director can save the situation. Pam asks her Turkish colleague if there is any way he can help. Within a few days, he has organised another supplier who can deliver even faster than the original supplier. He says: "I know that Brenda is honest and sincere. In my native village, we'd never leave someone like that in the lurch. It's a matter of honour."

It doesn't matter whether a person's idiosyncrasies are cultural or individual. Respect them and you will be rewarded. Richly.

Make the world a better place

The way Brenda deals with the dilemma does, of course, go a bit far. But then, that's why this is called the Advanced Level. Top people respond like that almost automatically. Not necessarily because they were brought up to do so, but because they recognised the need and taught themselves:

> The going is simply smoother and faster with fewer obstacles when you make an effort to understand other people. If you struggle to understand the culture, at least show respect and appreciation to save face.

That's something that mediocre teams just don't do. The excuse is: "No time!" That's nonsense. Regardless of whether you're being polite or impolite, a sentence will always take the same amount of time. Actually, you need less time for the politer version since your counterpart won't have to go into elaborate counter-attack or get defensive if you've accidentally stepped on his toes. What mediocre teams are really saying is: "We concentrate on the task at hand." That's ok, many people think like that. That has at least three disadvantages.

High performance can't be achieved with tunnel vision. For an intelligent human being it's not very intellectually satisfying to ignore cultures and individuals, or to tar them all with the same brush. That kind of ignorance about the world won't make the world a better place. Just imagine if we treated all individuals the way they'd like to be treated because we were aware of their cultural and individual peculiarities. Wouldn't that be fantastic?

In brief: Leading international teams

- Take stock of how intercultural idiosyncrasies are dealt with in your team: are you satisfied? Shocked? Appalled?
- Realise the impact cultural challenges can have on team climate, efficiency and performance.
- Address the issue of interculturality in your team! Do this at the kick-off and/or at regular intervals.
- Ask yourself and your team regularly: "What can we learn from each other?"
- Check whether the common team language is really understood and spoken by everybody.
- Where necessary, offer job-specific language courses (e-learning, at the very least, should be part of the standard packages for international project teams).
- Offer an introduction to the cultural backgrounds and characteristics of the countries which international project members come from. This is best done by hiring an external expert trainer. If that's not possible, delegate the task to one representative of each respective country.
- Focus of the cultural introduction: communication, implicit rules of business behaviour, and an understanding of how different virtues such as punctuality, quality, commitment are perceived.
- Emphasise in particular the differences between direct and indirect communication.
- Counter even the slightest symptoms of cultural egocentricity and prejudice whenever they raise their ugly heads!
- Establish a network of readily accessible and reliable country experts.
- With experience, you'll broaden your scope, and move from intercultural competence to individual, interpersonal competence: every person is unique both from a cultural and individual perspective. The more you are aware of this, the easier things will become.

"Speaking of 'the Americans' overlooks the 'American'".

Helen M., team leader

14. In medias res: The Chinese and the British

|||||||||||||||||||||||||||||||||||||||||||||||||||||

Just a quick stop-over

Let's not have any illusions about this: how many times have we heard, read, and participated in seminars about intercultural competence while making well-intentioned resolutions along the way? And has anything changed? See what I mean?

> The best way to learn to swim is by swimming. The same applies to acquiring intercultural competence: once learned, it's a skill that needs to be applied.

Good training does just that, and that's exactly what we intend to do as well, by exploring this central element of virtual leadership in more detail in the closing chapter. As case study examples, we'll refer to Chinese team members because of the increasing importance of that country; and British teams because they provide explicit and particularly salient examples of hidden intercultural pitfalls. As many Western European managers can be heard saying, "We all speak English, the Brits look just like us, they wear the same business clothes, they read the same books, they watch the same television. Their island isn't far away. They can't be that different. I really don't see a problem!" Wow! That's globalisation! Business has gone global, but personkind is still sitting in a cave in Altamira and scribbling on the walls. No one knows that better than Sabrina.

Sabrina is in charge of two strategic projects for a cosmetics company. Today she's arriving in New York to accept the milestone deliverables. After a one-hour meeting, everything is agreed upon and the responsible member of the steering committee gives the green light. Sabrina is on the next plane to Shanghai to meet with the directors of a company that is interested in a joint venture with her corporation.

After two hours, the Chinese partners are still engaged in a discussion about the best educational options for their children and ask Sabrina which nanny she has chosen for her two daughters. Sabrina is incensed: "Are they stringing us along? Do they have something to hide? We haven't made the slightest progress on the issue in the past two hours. What's going on? All I wanted to do is fly in and clarify the last open questions on the contract!" Sabrina just wanted to drop in briefly ... and found herself in a myriad of misunderstanding. She thinks the Chinese are out to sabotage the deal. They may even be negotiating with the competition. What do you think?

On the contrary, the Chinese are very keen on the joint venture, and consequently, they want to establish a personal, trust-based working relationship with Sabrina. That's why they talk about personal topics. They are thoroughly convinced that if you are going to commit to a longer-term collaboration then you had better get to know each other better! Sabrina has no intention of doing so. Her perspective is: "I need to close the deal and get the contract signed, then I'm out of here. The next important project is already waiting for me!" If the Chinese could read her mind, they'd break off negotiations immediately. The more they sense Sabrina's resistance to establishing a personal relationship, the more sceptical they become. Sabrina is in danger of causing the negotiations to collapse just a few yards short of the finish line! All because she is still too unfamiliar with the Chinese mindset.

When is direct too direct?

Alfred reports: "Meanwhile our Chinese team members deliver the kind of quality we need, but we still have some issues with on-time delivery. So, prior to the last delivery date, I told them point blank that I wouldn't accept another delay!" What happened next? Yep, the Chinese work package arrived three instead of two days too late. Alfred says: "They still don't get it! It looks like I'll have to be even more direct to make myself understood. Maybe I should threaten them with consequences!" Would you agree?

Under no circumstances! Blunt communication and threatening with consequences will get you nowhere in China. Generally speaking, the Chinese try to avoid confrontation. It's considered harmful, indecent and arrogant. Theoretically, Alfred knew that. But knowledge alone has never changed the world. The same can be said for most intercultural training courses. They are geared mainly toward transferring knowledge. That didn't help Alfred much. What did help: in the last training, the trainer had the group participate in intercultural simulations to increase intercultural sensitivity augmented by role plays and case studies to develop practical success strategies. That was really challenging, but after several role plays and a dozen or so case studies the participants felt more at ease at developing solutions for their given situations. The moral of the story: practice makes perfect.

Meanwhile, Alfred avoids every form of confrontation with his Chinese teammates. His motto is: "No more threats, blame and accusations! Instead:

emphasise commonalities and foster harmony. Once those elements are in place, I address the conflict in terms of a mutual problem that we'll solve together." Since he's changed his approach, the Chinese no longer sulk for days on end and are decidedly more punctual with their deliveries.

Yes means no

Marion heads an international design team. On the whole, she gets along reasonably well with all of her teammates. All, that is, except for the four Chinese colleagues at the Chinese industrial centre. They repeatedly deliver half-finished work and, as a result, have earned a reputation as 'unreliable'. How do you see it?

It's not that her Chinese colleagues are unreliable; they are simply overwhelmed. Often they are unable to fully complete their assigned tasks because they don't have the resources. So why don't they mention this when tasks are being delegated? Because saying 'no' is a no-go in China. From their perspective, their boss would lose face. That's why they don't say no. That is, of course they say no. They just don't use the actual word 'no'. So how do they do it? What does your intercultural competence tell you?

Marion has meanwhile honed her intercultural skills. She says: "I'm now familiar with at least half a dozen versions of a Chinese 'no'!" Before, when the Chinese team partner suddenly changed the subject in the middle of the discussion, other team members thought that extremely impolite. Today, everyone on the team knows: uh oh, that's a 'no' coming through. The Chinese are unable to carry out the task mentioned above, but they can't come out and say this directly. Instead, they say it implicitly by changing the subject. Sometimes they ignore part of the discussion or don't engage in the ongoing exchange. That, too, is as good as a 'no'. That's something we, in the West, need to become attuned to. In western cultures the old Roman adage prevails: silence means agreement. In China, often the opposite is true – the absolute opposite. It becomes really difficult if a Chinese team member says 'yes' and means 'no'. For example: "Yes, that's a good idea, but it may be a bit difficult to implement." A clear 'no' is couched in the very polite response to the idea, indicating that, from the Chinese side, its implementation will not work. Understanding these delicate nuances greatly reduces stress and improves chances of success in international teams. Conversely, it makes clear why international teams often rather struggle. And that, in polite Chinese terms, is putting it mildly.

Because every day hundreds if not thousands of international teams work hard at sabotaging themselves, most of them without even realising it. An Austrian team leader once said: "You assign work packages, then you get to work. We're used to working that way. When we expanded internationally and started working with the Chinese, it took us weeks to realise that some of the Asian colleagues had actually said 'no' while tasks were being assigned. It just didn't occur to us!" Meanwhile, valuable time has been wasted and can't be made up. Try to explain that to the customer or steering committee! And now, on to the British.

Typically British

We've already seen that the British tend to communicate more indirectly (see chapter 13). There's a lot of nodding in seminars with predominantly German participants when this subject comes up. As I explain: "You are German. That means what's absolutely straightforward for you comes across as impolite to a British person!" Suddenly, the nodding stops and reflection sets in:

What Germans consider rational and direct sounds impolite to many British people.

"Of course," Birgit says to Julie, "this can't work!" Julie flinches, but Birgit continues unperturbed: "First you must integrate the data from the new survey!" Julie thinks to herself: "Wait a minute, what's with the 'must'?" For Germans, 'must' simply means: do that and it will work! Julie being British, however, feels that she is being bossed around when she hears she 'must' do this or that. And hearing this from a German colleague ... that's unfortunate.

> **Politeness is a must. Must is not politeness.**

When Birgit realises this, she is momentarily shocked: "Sorry, Julie. I forgot myself. What I meant to say is: it happened to me, too. I got the wrong data; what a mess. I think you would find it very helpful, if you downloaded the new survey from our server." That's not exactly Oxford English, but it's softer and more relationship-focused enough that the British colleague doesn't dig her heels in. That makes sense, you say? Not to Birgit's male colleagues.

Their approach is: "Yes, but if I beat about the bush in this indirect way, the British won't realise how urgent the matter is!" The concern is understandable, but there is no need to worry. The British hear between the lines! They are finely attuned to such nuances. Take my word for it. So stop talking like a drill sergeant when you are leading an international team. And one more thing: forget another typically German pastime: factual consensus.

Factual consensus is overrated

Jürgen leaves the negotiation table in a state of total exhaustion, makes his way to the smoking area and lights up a cigarette. Inhaling deeply, he turns to the HR specialist standing next to him and says: "That British guy is driving me crazy! For hours now we've been trying to agree on how to launch an introduction campaign! He just won't go along with it! We're the ones who provided the budget! Doesn't he respect that?" Whereupon the HR specialist says: "I remember when I was in England that was one of the things that drove me nuts too. More puzzling for me, however, was that the Brits don't try to work through a stalemate. They simply say: 'We agree to disagree!'" Jürgen almost drops his cigarette in astonishment.

He re-joins the negotiation and says: "I think we can really refrain from forcing an agreement at this point. I'd merely like to ask you to go ahead with the media plan for the advertising campaign as discussed, please." "Sure, no worries," comes the prompt reply. The Brit gets to work without further ado. He's delighted that his German counterpart isn't insisting on a cut-and-dried agreement. What's much more important to him is maintaining a pleasant personal relationship. Although that doesn't mean you can expect a hug at the end of the meeting! Far from it!

Open displays of emotion are often 'just not done', especially in the business context. That goes for justified indignation and anger as much as outright joy or compassion. We all experience emotions, but please don't show them openly in public. Even if a British team member makes a disastrous mess of things, he isn't usually given a verbal dressing down (as might well happen in some other cultures). Instead, the tone remains polite. Otherwise, the manager would lose respect in the eyes of the team member and of the team. To the British, shouting often implies a lack of composure and leadership qualities. In Britain, the same applies to the opposite: one might be justifiably proud of an accomplishment; nevertheless, it should be kept to oneself. Emotions are not to be expressed publicly.

"That was awesome! Hey, we are the greatest!" People in many countries like to celebrate themselves and their success, and Americans are at the top of the list. If something goes well, celebrate immediately. The British find that rather embarrassing. Even if he/she were to win the Nobel Prize, "Thank you. How nice," is the epitome of what you'll hear in terms of an emotional outburst, while people from other cultures might be breaking open the champagne in celebratory exuberance or shouting from the rooftops. So show a little empathy for your British colleague! That's not asking too much is it?

The British 'no' and British humour

"I'm sorry but I really feel …" Or: "I don't feel altogether comfortable with that." What does that mean? It means 'No'. Many continental Europeans don't hear the nuance, get the wrong end of the stick and complain bitterly afterwards: "Why can't they just say no when they mean no?" They do! They just do it very, very carefully.

A British team member once mailed all his team colleagues a 'bilingual' version of a rejection of another team member's recommendation: "For the English: I'm sorry. I'm afraid I'm having difficulty going along with this proposal. I'm just wondering if perhaps we should give it some more thought. For the Germans: *Nein!*"

Continental Europeans often get confused at how vehemently the normally so reserved Brits can dish out humour. Unfortunately, such misunderstandings have even ended up in court, such as in the case of a British team member caricaturing the German team leader by goose-stepping down the hall, sporting a clipped moustache and combat boots and shouting indecipherable Teutonic orders. Whether you find this funny or not, it probably shouldn't really end up in a courtroom. British humour can be both very subtle and at the same time quite tough. Especially if it's part of the Forming ritual (chapter 5). For the British, it's important not to take yourself too seriously; to be adept at skilful bantering, and to be able to dish out and take flak. All newcomers are expected to run that humorous, ritual gauntlet. This is the team baptism of fire, so to speak. Those who pass earn respect. Those who feel insulted, sulk or run for help, lose trust and credibility.

The magic bullet

What's the difference between teams with a high level of intercultural competence and a low level? That can be explained in two words: intercultural awareness. Teams that have a low level of intercultural competence tend to continually underestimate the problems caused by interculturality. Competent teams, on the other hand, are aware of the challenge. I'm often asked for the secret weapon on how to deal with this issue. I point out that they're already using the secret weapon just by expressing an active interest and asking for my advice:

> Actively practising intercultural awareness is the magic weapon!

That means: constantly encouraging your team to be aware of often hidden cultural differences and idiosyncrasies well in advance of an actual intercultural encounter, and setting an example by practising what you preach. Remind them to avoid knee-jerk reflexes triggered by their own cultural conditioning. Instead, delay judgement, show appreciation; focus on commonalities and mutual understanding. By the way, this magic bullet is not only a recipe for success in international teams!

It also works in your own department, relationships, marriage and family life. In fact, in all of these areas where we often behave like a bull in a china shop. Here, it's not the cultural idiosyncrasies as much as the personal ones. We often overlook the needs of those closest to us, show little empathy, steer clear of difficult conversations, and then wonder why our employees are not motivated, the kids don't respect us, the dog doesn't obey, and significant others keep their distance.

> Awareness and dealing mindfully with intercultural and interpersonal idiosyncrasies is the key to success not only for international teams.

Those are beautiful closing words.

Epilogue to the elegance of excellence

In closing, here's a great word of comfort: you can probably forget everything you've just read. In fact, you can forget the entire book. Because when we look at team leadership in actual practice, conditions are often so chaotic and disastrous that nobody would notice if the way you managed your team was terrible too. On the contrary, you'd be fitting into the norm. I know, nobody would say that out loud.

I am saying it out loud. Because I witness this situation every day: mediocrity rules. People moan about it, but in the end they all seem to come to terms with it. Well, obviously you haven't because it seems you're still here. What does 'here' mean? You're on your way to excellence, and that deserves high praise indeed in our age of mediocrity. You want to do it better. I congratulate and honour you for that. How do you make it happen?

By just doing it. I'm not joking. For heaven's sake, don't try and put this whole book into practice all at once; there is enough in here to clobber a small elephant. Start with the smallest of steps. Some team leaders hand out copies of the book to members of their team; others copy pages of the parts they find most essential or put them on the intranet so they can be discussed at the next meeting: "Is that something we'd be interested in doing? Is there something we want to improve?" Those are small, manageable steps to get the ball rolling on the road to change.

Change happens in small and manageable steps.

The notion of a quantum leap is a myth that has never been scientifically proven. Even if there are exceptions, they are exceptions. A team leader with a PhD in chemistry said: "I'm so focused on test results and data that my teams really don't like working with me. Now I've decided to spend at least a minute at the beginning of each phone call, and at least ten minutes during meetings, talking about how people are, what's new, and even just about the weather!" Tiny steps?

Certainly. Still, it wasn't easy after 20 years in the job to switch from focusing purely on the task at hand to topics that are relevant to the well-being of the team. In the first two phone calls she promptly 'forgot' her 'small' step. It was too much of a transformation for her. So here's my transfer and change tip:

Give yourself and your next small step nine fair chances!

What does that mean? Well, advertising experts found out that on average (!), a consumer has to be confronted with a new product physically or in the form of advertising at least nine times before he considers buying it (impulse buying not included). That's why repeated marriage proposals are often effective sooner or later. At this point in seminars, often one of the participants says, "That's true, he/she finally accepted after the fourth proposal!" So, give yourself at least nine tries before you give up! It works a lot faster if you involve your team.

Get your team together or send them an e-mail: "You know, the distance between us makes things rather complicated and time-consuming. I've been thinking about something we could do to bridge the distance, and would like to hear your opinion. What do you think if we …?" I know, this might lead to another tough discussion in your team, I realise that. Change requires a lot of time and nerves, and leads some to believe it's better to give up and leave things as they are. You don't agree? Why not?

For two good reasons. First, because you want to improve; you hate stagnation and mediocrity. Secondly, because wanting to and being able to do a better job is more fun and contributes to a feeling of success. Both are powerful motives. Keep the faith. Many people are quite happy to live with mediocrity. You are obviously not one of them. Remember a great team leader in history and what he had to say to that. Shakespeare (in Hamlet) said: "This above all: to thine own self be true." Stay true to the motives that drive you. It will impact your teams positively. I can promise you that. If you would like help with developing your skills further, I'll be happy to assist you. Anywhere in the world. Drop me a line anytime. Here's where you can reach me:

Gary Thomas
Thomas@international-hr.de
www.international-hr.de

About the author

In his role as Managing Director of assist International Human Resources, Gary Thomas has been involved in delivering coaching, training and consulting projects across the globe for many years. His clients are international corporations, medium sized-companies and global start-ups.

His particular focus is international leadership, virtual leadership, intercultural competence development and train-the trainer programmes.

Born in England, Gary lives with his wife and two children in Germany.

The portfolio of assist International Human Resources:

- International Business Skills Training
- International Soft Skills Training
- Intercultural Coaching
- Cross-Culture Coaching Plus
- Intercultural Workshops
- Intercultural Train The Trainer programmes
- Blended Learning on the assist Virtual Campus

Contact:

assist International HR
A division of assist GmbH
Technologiepark 12
33100 Paderborn
Germany

www.international-hr.de
Tel.:+49 5251 87543-2
Contact@international-hr.de

www.ingramcontent.com/pod-product-compliance
Lightning Source LLC
Chambersburg PA
CBHW021517210326
41599CB00012B/1294